Anatoly Gladilin / THE MAKING AND UNMAKING OF A SOVIET WRITER: MY STORY OF THE "YOUNG PROSE" OF THE SIXTIES AND AFTER. Translated by David Lapeza. Published by *ARDIS / ANN ARBOR*

ardis / ann arbor

ISBN 0-88233-354-2 (cloth)
ISBN 0-88233-355-0 (paperback)

Library of Congress Catalog Card No. 78-74199

Published by Ardis
2901 Heatherway
Ann Arbor, Michigan 48104

CONTENTS

THE MAKING AND UNMAKING OF A SOVIET WRITER

I

I am not a politican, I am a writer. In Moscow
when we argued endlessly about the peculiarities—to
put it mildly—of the authorities in our country, it
seemed there was a lot to say on the subject—more
than enough for one lifetime. Now, when I've finally
gained complete freedom of speech—say whatever you
like—I feel rather shy. Why? I'll try to explain. In
Moscow, coming out on political issues (i.e., signing—
not too often—some letter from the Sakharov Committee for the Protection of Human Rights) or speaking
out (now and then) on the rostrum at a Union of
Writers meeting, I knew that we were playing on equal
terms with the authorities. That is, I could express the
usual "seditious slander" and the authorities, in turn,
could employ (if they pleased) repression in regard to
me. Now I am in Paris, I am in safety. How can the
authorities answer me? Well, *The Literary Gazette*[1] will
publish some libel about the appearance of yet another
emigré "pouring out buckets of filth on the nation of
triumphant socialism." What's it to me? On the contrary, it's almost an honor—it means it got to them, it
means it hit the mark. And still it is a wildly unusual
position: to be able to express one's ideas and not be
punished for it.

Apparently, I am, to use the Marxist phrase, a
typical product of my time. I lived in the USSR for

[11]

forty years, I have Soviet brains. I make no secret of the fact that it's not easy for me to say "mister" instead of "comrade." I still warily expect some "agent of a certain foreign intelligence service" could come and ask me to sell the plans of a Soviet factory. Under pressure, I could sketch a plan of the bakery and grocery store closest to my home in Moscow, however I swear I would never do it—that's how I was brought up.

I know precisely how things should not be in our country. With less confidence am I able to set out how things should be. But how, in what manner could it come about? Here too I am silent. So many variants, so many diametrically opposed points of view—that's politics—and I'm not a politician, I'm a writer.

It's probably too late for me to change professions. Stendahl said that literature is a mirror on a highway. Whatever happens on the road, literature reflects, shows us, and you, dear readers, examine, if you're not too lazy, the picture recorded and interpret it as you understand it. Actually, I always worked that way. There are ten of my books in Russia with editions totaling 800,000 copies. Undoubtedly some of my stories will seem naive now. But I'll answer for any of my books. They were written honestly. That is just what I thought at the time—I was a mirror, I reflected...

The most curious thing was that up to the moment of my departure from the USSR, I was in the position of a "successful" writer. It's even sort of strange...

I've been in literature for twenty years. My first stories were printed in a popular magazine (and, naturally, lent it popularity) with a circulation of 100,000, a half million, a million. I confess, I liked it when I boarded a subway car and saw at least two people reading my piece. I was recognized on the street, I was invited to writers' conferences, the central press wrote about my books (damning more often than praising them); and it was a normal, and as I now understand it, a happy life. It went on that way for ten years.

Every writer believes in his own talent. It cannot be otherwise. Who will believe in you if you doubt yourself? But now, soberly evaluating my first steps in literature (and, naturally, not rejecting any of the above in the least), I suspect I was awfully lucky. I began in 1956, when we all thought we had woken from a terrible dream and, of course, would correct all the mistakes of the past (if not right away, then gradually), and the country would set off on a different path. My ideas tallied with those of my contemporaries. I was a mirror, I reflected. And for the authorities, my books (particularly in light of these circumstances— plus the youth and naiveté of the author) were comparatively acceptable. Don't forget that in those years the so-called liberalization of society was going on.

But ten years later they had already "closed me down." Not a single magazine would print me anymore. To judge by literary criticism, there was in Soviet literature no writer Gladilin, no "confessional prose," no "city novel," the beginnings of which were tied to my name.

Chased from the door, I climbed in the window. Five years later, in the genre of the historical novel, I managed to publish *The Gospel According to Robespierre*. Surprisingly enough, this novel was distributed by Politizdat, the publishing house of the Party Central Committee, in the series "Flaming Revolutionaries." In the same series they put out novels by Trifonov, Aksenov, Voinovich, Kornilov, and Okudzhava. Many of these books were surprises for the reader—either in their content or in the offensiveness of their authors' names. In short, they published my novel, and in reward there were questions from the readers—how could they let it through?—and almost complete silence from the critics. But nothing I have written on contemporary themes in the last decade has seen the light of day in my homeland. (What a long time for literature—ten years! And it was precisely in my capacity as "mirror" that I felt so strong.)

However—in 1975 my second historical novel, *Dreams of Schlüsselburg Fortress,* came out; Soviet Writer Publishing House put out a collection of old pieces (once they were no longer considered dangerous), and even Children's Publishing House[2] published an adventure story. Three books in one year! A record for a mere Soviet mortal! And the press remembered me. Reviews were ordered, they were to have appeared...

How could I leave? At very least I was a well-known writer in my own country. But in the "accursed West" no one knows me, and specialists maintain that in general, Western readers have only heard of Dostoevsky and Solzhenitsyn from all of Russian literature.

But I left.

Why?

I shall try to answer that question briefly.

It is my deep conviction that no real writer, no Russian writer would leave Russia. He would not leave, no matter how badly he lived in his homeland, no matter what goodies he was promised abroad, if he had the possibility of at least occasionally publishing his books in the country. For no matter how the manuscript is warped by Soviet censors and by the editors (and they are practically the same thing), the book retains that explosive reserve which undermines the foundations of the totalitarian state. The coefficient of effective action of a "modest," but honest, story is much higher than that of a "teethrattling" political pamphlet published abroad. Debatable question? Probably. But in Russia, a good book instantly disappears from the counter, it is read by hundreds of thousands, and foreign publications penetrate the cordon in single copies. *C'est la vie,* as the French say.

Those leave who are sent out. Those leave who can no longer do anything in their country.

All of my books that could possibly be published I forced through. With the other manuscripts I persistently knocked on the doors of publishing houses and magazines. It sometimes happened that with the aid of friends and "connoisseur-patrons" my books were put on the typesetting schedule. I saw the dress rehearsals of my plays. One performance was even recorded on videotape for television. But nothing made it to the reader or viewer. I understood that I could no longer outwit the authorities. And of course, whatever else I wanted to write and was able to write—would not get anywhere.

Further. Unlike his professional colleague abroad, the Soviet writer (more precisely: I speak only of our real writers—I will not touch on the literary gangsters, of which we have cultivated a great many, on principle; it's not worth mentioning them)—the Soviet writer is burdened mainly with a single problem: to find a theme, an angle on "our wonderful reality," so that on the one hand he can tell about it honestly, and on the other have a chance of publishing the manuscript. An agonizing dilemma. And so much strength and energy is spent on these hourly, daily battles with the superior forces of the editorial-censorship machinery. And these engagements last years for every manuscript! Twenty years I lived by the rules foisted upon me by the literary *oprichina*[3] in control. And suddenly a simple idea occurred to me: perhaps enough is enough? What if one were to try speaking loud and clear and send both external and internal editors to hell? (Yes, in each of us sits our own internal censor—I repeat, all of us our products of our time...) It won't work? Well, you'll have only yourself to blame, and you won't be able to hide behind external circumstances, or sit up in the House of Writers[4] like a venerable classic crying in your beer and muttering "bastards, swine, scum, vermin, why I could have... eh, Vanya, run to the bar and get another half-liter." Honestly, I have the impression that if right now I were sitting quietly at home, had not gone off anywhere, and had even stopped writing altogether, my earlier published books would have been quite enough for me to be canonized as a "Soviet classic" in about five years, and in ten years, to grace solemn writers' presidiums with my presence, puff out my cheeks and try my hardest to make myself out as a "father of the Russian intelligentsia."

Of course, I would have manuscripts in my desk which, probably after my death, would play a slightly different tune. But when would that be, and would it be? But in the meantime, it would turn out that I had played the hand foisted upon me by the State, that I had submitted and, having earned my pound of goodies, closed my eyes to the rest. They don't bother me, I'm loyal, it's no concern of mine...

No! A buttered prick for them!

However my literary career develops now, whatever disappointments await me in the future, in my opinion, I've managed to accomplish my primary social function. By my example, Sofia Vlasievna[5] is once more convinced that writers cannot be bought! And that's the most important thing.

And then we in Russia are used to stewing in our own juice. We've lost our point of comparison. You write better than Sofronov or Mikhail Alexeev[6] —that's really good, you're practically a genius. But there was a great Russian literature in the nineteenth century! What about us? Have we moved forward or fallen back? Let's look about "objectively and exactingly." Well, if there are any writers among us who consider themselves as talented as Gogol or Tolstoy—let them speak up! What are they afraid of?

And how does our literature look on a professional level next to American or English literature? The "decaying West" hasn't been standing still, damn it.

That's what Russian writers ought to think about first.

Yes, we have wonderful prose (I speak only of the dead, so as not to start quarrels among the living)—the prose of Bulgakov and Platonov, Mandelstam and Babel, and of the emigrants—Bunin and Nabokov. But Russia is a huge country; and with such a glorious literary tradition! Isn't that awfully little?

This is, doubtless, a very debatable and comlex argument. Let us return to it another time. However, just now, for completely understandable and valid reasons, in our country a book's value, in the majority of cases, is defined by the principles: what is it about, what new information has the author conveyed, how bold is he..." I repeat, all of this is extremely important and necessary.

But there are other, eternal criteria in literature:
(1) what is the moral position of the author?
(2) how does he write?

Most likely, it would be very immodest for writers who have emigrated to rend their shirts and cry, "Only we are trying, we shall not bring shame to the land of Rus," etc.

Nevertheless, everything else being equal, a qualitative leap in our prose, poetry, drama, criticism, and journalism is more likely under conditions of free creativity and a free literature.

I have attempted briefly to answer the simple question of why I left. However, I feel that I've managed to touch only a few aspects of a sore and stirring subject: why do we have a talent and brain drain from our country?

Critical analysis of events may not be my strong point. So I shall try to tell as objectively as possible of the literary events in which I myself participated and of my comrades, who are, probably, more talented and better-known in our country than I. Objectively? Well, that won't work. With Bella Akhmadulina, I say:

> Let's be partial to our friends,
> Let's think they're wonderful...
> Losing them is awful. God forfend.[7]

II

Just try to find a living soul who would agree to read the works of Fyodor Gladkov, Panferov, Pavlenko, Perventsev, Koptyaeva, Seifullina. No one is that stupid. Well, for a suitable remuneration, then of course; ultimately men must do even more onerous work to earn money. But before 1956 these writers were considered classics. Their books were studied in school. People really read them. What could you do? There were no others. The average in Soviet literature then was about on the level of Babaevsky's novel *Knight of the Golden Star.*

True, there were still Maxim Gorky, Fadeev, Sholokhov, Ehrenburg, Kataev, Kaverin. However, the average Soviet reader believed the newspapers, the critics, the school syllabus. And they persistently advanced the idea that one had to approach the works of these writers differentially. So, for example, of Gorky's books the novel *Mother* was emphasized (in my opinion, his weakest work) and "The Maiden and Death," which Comrade Stalin considered "better than Goethe's *Faust,*" while the novel *Klim Samgin* was always kept in the shade. All of my contemporaries have written more than one essay on Fadeev's *The Young Guard,* and knew both variants of the novel.[1] Few read his best tale "The Rout." So of the gold reserves of Soviet literature, the works least successful in their artistic

[19]

qualities but most ideologically consistent were propagandized. Perhaps this was just only in relation to Sholokhov—as far as I know, no one has disputed the authorship of *Virgin Soil Upturned.*[2] *It is nece*ssary to add here that the general reader simply did not know the names of Bulgakov, Platonov, Mandelstam, Babel.

There is no rule without an exception. After the war, Viktor Nekrasov's novella *In the Trenches of Stalingrad,* Emmanuel Kazakevich's *The Star,* Vera Panova's *Fellow-travelers,* Yury Trifonov's *Students* were very popular. But these books were drops in a sea of dull hack literature.

In the literary market, as in any other, demand determines supply. It was not at all necessary for a writer to search for new forms, an individual style, or artistic imagery; and of course, it was absolutely forbidden to have new ideas. A writer was required (and I quote), "to be guided by the principles of Communist Party-spirit, by a Marxist-Leninist-Stalinist worldview, and truthfully to reflect socialist reality in the spirit of socialist realism."[3] If we translate this hocus-pocus into Russian, the basic criterion for publication of a manuscript was the following: how loudly the author shouted "hurrah!" and most important, with what zeal he glorified "the wise leader and teacher, the Soviet gymnasts' best friend."

As for the truthful reflection of reality, here's an example from the "classics" of the time: in Vasily Azhaev's novel *Far From Moscow,* an oil refinery is built by free workers, not convicts. Through the pages of Semyon Babaevsky's books stroll well-fed, millionaire kolkhoz workers, while in reality the countryside was kicking off from hunger. So the writer was supposed to tell not of the reality that actually existed, but of how it should be. That showed the spirit of socialist realism.

We grew up in the era of the struggle against "cosmopolitanism, servility, the cult of the foreign."[4] The works of Zoshchenko and Akhmatova were represented as symbols of moral decay and ideological depravity. For us, the newly discovered Christ-martyr figure was the narrow-minded Pavka Korchagin.[5] From infancy it was drummed into our heads that the true example, worthy of imitation for youth was, and would always be, the informer Pavlik Morozov.[6] And the outlook was for a future literature of the nation of triumphant socialism where there could arise only conflicts between "the good and the better."

In the theater, they gave the green light to the Surovys, Korneichuks and Sofronovs. All the working class families on stage had stylish apartments in skyscrapers with the obligatory view of the Kremlin stars.

And in poetry... I don't pretend to give an objective analysis, I'm trying to remember. Yes, we loved Mayakovsky, Bagritsky, Utkin, and read a little Esenin and Blok on the sly, but for the rest of our lives each of us bears within himself the clichéd lines: "With gentle light does morning redden the Kremlin's ancient walls," "In the vastness of our marvelous homeland,/ Tempered in battle and toil,/ We composed a joyous song/ Of our great friend and leader," "Gunners, Stalin gave the order,/ Gunners, the Fatherland calls," "Of Stalin, wise, paternal and beloved,/ The people write wonderful songs," "We're all for peace—all peoples sing this song,/ We're all for peace, let the corn ripen..." "Komsomol boys are restless souls,/ Komsomol boys get the job done," and of course, "A new China marches beside us" and "Stalin and Mao are listening."

That's the sort of picture the literary "cornfield" of the post-war era presented. In it dogmatists, hacks and incompetents freely gamboled, regularly received Stalin Prizes, and built dachas "behind the blue fence."[7] But normal people's reaction to this literary bacchanal was always the same: they borrowed fewer and fewer books by Soviet writers from the libraries, and more and more Russian and foreign classics.

I catch myself on the thought suddenly—aren't I mistaken, carried away by generalizations? Perhaps it is only now that the past seems do dark to me, while actually everything was quite different? I shall try to remember what I read myself in those years. I should note that I was an ordinary guy, and wasn't thinking of a literary career, but dreamed of entering the airforce pilots' school. Let's see, I loved Lermontov and Gogol, Balzac and Dickens. I didn't like Tolstoy and Turgenev much because we covered them intensively in school, and everything covered in school provoked hatred. Like all of my contemporaries, I quoted Ilf and Petrov by heart. I knew only excerpts from Dostoevsky (that "obscurantist and reactionary" was still banned then).[8] For some reason I was interested in foreign authors, although it was difficult to get your bearings among the thousands of unfamiliar names. You see, they recommended to us only the progressive writers and those of procommunist tendency. I remember hearing somewhere about Sigmund Freud, and asking for one of his books in the Lenin Library.[9] The librarian's face turned red. "You ought to be ashamed, young man!" the librarian cried angrily. "Reading such pornography!"

I admit I was frightened, although I didn't know what pornography was. But as I figure it now, the librarian didn't know what Freud was.

The poems in the newspapers dispelled any desire to read poetry. As for the works of contemporary Soviet writers, I, with the maximalism of youth then

[22]

characteristic of me, sincerely believed that if one were to gather them in one pile, drench them with kerosene and set them on fire, literature could only benefit.

In tenth grade we learned by heart that wise dictum of Comrade Malenkov's: "The typical is a political phenomenon." I confess that I simply could not understand the perspicacity of this remark, although later it was explained to me that Comrade Malenkov didn't think it up himself, but simply filched it from someone.[10] I repeat, I'm a writer, and not a politician. I shall try to sketch a typical portrait of my contemporary, the contemporary of many other writers of my generation. But if unexpectedly, political tendency becomes noticeable in this portrait, honestly, I'm not guilty; submit all claims to the comrade leaders.

Petya Ivanov, or Vanya Petrov, the Russian version of an ordinary Joe Doakes, was born in 1933-1938, in Moscow, Leningrad, Tambov... Primarily an urbanite, primarily a Russian. During the war he was evacuated to Kazan, Novosibirsk, Tashkent, and terribly envious of his older brothers, who returned from the front with orders and medals.

In Moscow, Leningrad, Tambov, Petya Ivanov or Vanya Petrov, lived in a communal apartment,[11] teased the neighbors' cat, shot his sling shot in the courtyards, stood in line for flour.

Sometimes, Petya Ivanov didn't have a father or mother. Either they died during the war or they were somewhere else, but where exactly—one did not ask. In answer to indiscreet questions, relatives would shush threateningly: "Quiet, the neighbors will hear."

Petya Ivanov, primarily urbanite, primarily Russian, grew up a patriotically inclined, loyal citizen, and liked to march with Papa or Mama in holiday demonstrations on November 7th and the 1st of May.[12]

Muscovite Petya Ivanov was really lucky once—he saw Stalin on the rostrum of the mausoleum—a small withered old man with the nicest smile, not at all like his portraits and photographs.

On summer vacation, Petya Ivanov was sent to Pioneer camps where in the festive campline he sang "Soar up, like bonfires in the blue night,/ We are Pioneers, workers' children," and after lights-out, quite different songs, but also traditional at Pioneer camps: "Bill's back from northern Canada,/ Hey, boys, pour the wine,/ We'll drink to tender Mary,/ it's near a year that she's been true..."

In the seventh or eighth grade, Petya Ivanov wrote an essay on the book *How the Steel was Tempered* and entered the Komsomol. Petya Ivanov was a Spartacus, Dynamo or CCRA fan,[13] knew he lived in the capitalist encirclement and sincerely sympathized with the bitter fate of foreign workers, especially the Blacks in America.

The "accursed West" was constantly decaying. Every year the final, decisive crisis was expected, which would completely wipe capitalism from the face of the earth. Petya believed the newspapers, but in the newspapers one found miracles time and again: today's chairman of a fraternal Communist Party turns out to be a vile bourgeois hireling. But then, Petya Ivanov primarily read the fourth page, where the sports column was.[14] If some radical problem did bother Petya, it was only the question of coeducation.[15]

Like all the Soviet people, Petya Ivanov took hard the death of the Great Leader and Teacher on March 5, 1953. Muscovite Petya Ivanov was lucky once again: he broke through the wild crush and throng almost to the doors of the Column Hall in the House of Unions[16] whence, half-suffocated, unconscious, he was conveyed by ambulance to Sklifasovsky Institute.

The spirit of heterodoxy in Petya Ivanov began to come through at high school parties, when they made him dance only ball room dances—the *pas d'espagne* or butterfly polka—and categorically forbid groping through a fox trot or tango. The *druzhinniki*[17] would stop Petya on the street and cut his narrow trousers to shreds. "Why can't I dress as I like!" wondered Petya Ivanov, exasperated.

On the kolkhoz, they gave out rotten cabbage for work-days;[18] in the camps, millions of political prisoners languished; but Petya Ivanov knew nothing of all that, though he did know that the country was waging a bitter war with *stilyagi*.[19]

In June 1954, Lavrenty Pavlovich Beria, "loyal friend and colleague of the great leader and teacher," suddenly turned out to be an Anglo-Americano-Japanese spy; and even earlier there were rumors that the murderer-doctors[20] weren't guilty at all, and beggars in the trams sang "What have you done, Lidka Timashuk?" That's when Petya Ivanov started thinking long and seriously.

Tourists started coming from the "rotting West," not at all like exhausted unfortunates. Import clothes were the fashion. Petya Ivanov was much aggrieved: how was he supposed to get a foreign jacket with ten roubles in his pocket?

Just then, reports began to filter down that our glorious laboring peasantry weren't living well at all... and that there had been some exaggerations, shortcomings and deficiencies...

And 1956 arrived, when it was no longer necessary to outline and memorize Chapter Four of the *Short Course*[21] when "the great continuer of a great doctrine" himself turned out to be...

It never rains but it pours.

Petya Ivanov wasn't at all like Hamlet, but at this point he uttered the famous Shakespearian phrase, "Something is rotten in Denmark (i.e., the Soviet Union)!" Hence he came to the conclusion that from now on we could not take anyone at their word—we had to try to live by our wits.

Like every Soviet citizen, Petya Ivanov religiously believed in the bases of socialism and simply figured that some individual mistakes had been made, which we would now, of course, correct, if not right away, then gradually. Alas, the naive Petya Ivanov did not suspect that having once decided to live by his wits, he had chosen a seditious path, leading to heterodoxy and dissidence. Verily was Comrade Malenkov correct: the typical became a political phenomenon.

I repeat, Petya Ivanov retained a great many illusions, but when Soviet tanks rumbled down the streets of Budapest, the capital of Soviet Socialist Hungary, Petya Ivanov understood that the rest of his life was not going to be strewn with roses.

Petya Ivanov clenched his fists, hid his hands in his pockets and gave them the finger. As yet, this was his first revolt against the authorities...

III

After tenth grade, I went off to Kazakhstan to enter the military academy of the Air Fighter Command. A Soviet upbringing will show—even now I cannot give the exact address of the academy, I'm so used to keeping military secrets. However, in the quarantine station of the city of N—, I ran up against the army face to face for the first time, and instantly all the romance disappeared. In the army, personalities were not needed, the army needed obedient automatons. And then I understood that my true calling wasn't flying anyway, it was writing.

I returned to Moscow, but was too late for the competitive exams for the institutes. But then, it is uncertain I would have gotten through the competition successfully—for most of my contemporaries didn't get in the institutes. Yes, "the times of Viktor Podgursky" began with a sharp reduction in admissions to institutions of higher education.

I got fixed up as an electromechanics student at... (so now this is a military secret too, even if the apparently peaceful enterprise made machine tools?... Damn them and their secrets!)—in short, I worked days, and wrote in the evening. I regularly sent my stories off to various journals, and just as regularly they sent them back with harsh reviews, all but telling me to go to hell. But in summer 1954, I managed to get in the Gorky Literary Institute of the Union of Writers of the USSR. The competition was stiff, thirty for every place. Why did they take me? I don't know. If someone dug up one of my old stories, I'd probably hang myself from shame.

At the end of the school year, my "works" were discussed in the seminar and I was panned thoroughly, but the administration decided to be lenient with me and let me stay in the institute until fall. I remember I came out of the seminar completely stunned; it was drizzling outside and in my head buzzed the first lines of "The Chronicle of the Times of Viktor Podgursky." I finished this novella in a month, published it a year later in *Youth (Iunost')* magazine, and the question of my expulsion from the institute was no longer brought up.

"The Chronicle of the Times of Viktor Podgursky"... Literary heroes of the time usually sat at Komsomol meetings, criticizing conceited *stilyagi* who, as a rule, drove around in their Daddy's Pobeda.[1] True, there were innovations: the hero of Viktor Rozov's play *Good Luck!*, with his family and personal life muddled up, solved all his problems at one stroke and went off to the building sites of communism! Over the radio, young voices sang the cheerful song, "We have come at dawn, one by one, on passes from the Komsomol. Friends, let's go to far off parts, pioneers let's be—you and me..." Across the screen ambled rosy-cheeked, well-fed youths, who, in the finale, turn up on Red Square with girls in white ball gowns, and loudly thank "the wise Party, who opened to youth all the roads of life."

I read these books, listened to the songs, watched the movies... and choked with indignation. It was all lies, fake. For my contemporaries, everything was different. Life greeted us with a sock in the mouth. From infancy it was drummed into us that a high-school diploma was a ticket to life. And here it was in our hands. We want to study, we want to have some worthy profession—if not, then out of the path! I understand that now, with the distance of time, our misfortunes then seem petty, but youth has its own dramas, its own tragedies...

The title of my story itself was polemical. Earlier, they wrote chronicles of kings, and later, after the Revolution, "chronicles of the fiery years," or of some other great events. But wouldn't you like to read the chronicle of the times of an ordinary fellow? I mean, look at life as yesterday's high school student, Viktor Podgursky, saw it? I set myself no more grandiose task. I simply wanted to show life as it was. And my characters did not express themselves in fancy literary language, but spoke the living language of the street. That's all, actually.

"The Chronicle" lay in the files of *Youth* for a year. In general, as I understand it, a year is the normal period for a manuscript to get through a Soviet journal. Especially since no one was in a hurry with "The Chronicle," after all, the author was known to absolutely no one. *Youth* magazine was just barely on its feet. They printed venerable authors, recognized specialists on problems of youth, though the only things published in the journal that had been successful were Adamov's detective story *The Florid File* and Thor Heyerdahl's report on sailing the Kon-Tiki. "The Chronicle" moved slowly through each editorial stage. Each editor in turn diligently lit into the story, basically striking out the slang and pointed street expressions. It's uncertain how long all this would have continued; but luckily for me, a protectress turned up—the head of the magazine's prose section. I'll be grateful to her to the grave. In short, she seized the moment and slipped the story to Valentin Kataev.

Usually, after lectures at the Literary Institute, I'd go to the magazine, and no one paid any attention to me. They were used to having some bum in a ragged jacket hanging around... And then, one fine day, upon my arrival, they all poured out into the hall; they were all congratulating me! It turned out that the editor-in-chief himself, Valentin Petrovich Kataev *wept*, reading "The Chronicle." The story was added to the very next issue. Undoubtedly Kataev liked the story, but I don't think he found anything special in it; he just decided to play the hooligan—to show his venerable authors that, see, here's a twenty-year-old guy who writes no worse than you do. But what was the amazement of the editorial board and Kataev himself, when at the first readers' conference the speakers talked only of "The Chronicle." And at later conferences too, the history of Viktor Podgursky was the center of attention. The editorial board was flooded with readers' comments; they wrote more about "The Chronicle" than all the other pieces put together. The issue with "The Chronicle" instantly disappeared from the book counters. People said that high school and college students read the story right during class, tore it out of each others' hands. And, at last, the central press responded...

Seven years later in the assembly hall of a large institute, I was at one of my regular receptions with my readers. And again, almost all of the speakers mentioned "The Chronicle." A literary critic, who was chairing the conference, whispered in my ear, "Tolya, I reread 'The Chronicle' recently. In my opinion, it's weak, and only at the end is it apparent that the author isn't as big a fool as he seems at first." It's quite likely that the critic was right, however "The Chronicle"

[30]

made a breach in the official Soviet classics. My literary contemporaries, the well-known writers of the future, could see for themselves, that as it turns out, you can write that way too.

It's a difficult, indeed almost impossible task for a writer to evaluate his own book fairly. When it's published, a book begins to live its own separate life. Those who so desire can reread "The Chronicle of the Times of Viktor Podgursky," but I have a special attitude towards this, my first story. With age you get sentimental.

IV

And so, quite unexpectedly, at twenty-one I became a famous writer. Schools and colleges invited me to discussions of "The Chronicle of the Times of Viktor Podgursky." What's more, I could allow myself the luxury of not attending the creative writing seminar for my class. And they all excused me. Naturally: a graduate of the Literary Institute usually received a diploma with distinction if he got just one of his short stories published, and here a third-year student has a novella in a major magazine... The Institute's administration had something to brag about—we reared him, we educated him!

But I remember well that I did not reap the fruits of fame. I was in an abominable mood; I worked a lot, couldn't sleep at night, but my second book—"The Brigantine Raises Sail"—was scarcely moving.

Yes, I had typically Soviet brains. The press blared on about the glorious deeds of our youth at the building sites of communism. How could I, a young writer, not go to Siberia, "not join in, not be inspired?" And therefore, in the summer of 1956, when "The Chronicle" had been scheduled for publication, I set off for the Altai, to the Biisk artillery plant, then under construction.[1]

Naturally, I tried my hardest to hide the fact that I was a man of letters. I lived in a dormitory with the workers. For some reason, I was immediately nominated to the Komsomol committee. So I didn't argue, it allowed me to spend time in every area. Alas, as before, it was as if some evil fate got me down. In the clash with actual reality, all romance was completely shattered. I saw that the guys from Moscow and Leningrad had come to Biisk with the best of intentions. They "were sick of talks and fights" in the stifling communal apartments of the capitals; and they hoped that not "on the far, filibusterous Black Sea," but here in the expanses of the Altai, "the brigantine would raise sail." They sought a truly worthy life. They were ready for primitive surroundings. But they got the dirty work, they were cheated on their pay, and the press, instead of helping the Komsomol volunteers, lied shamelessly.

I don't deny that I came to Biisk with the outline of a future novella ready. I dreamed of repeating the success of "The Chronicle," but "The Brigantine" just didn't want to raise sail. The "Altai material" wouldn't listen, and led me off in completely the wrong direction. I wasn't a very experienced man of letters, but fully realized that not only would a book like that not bring official success—simply no one would publish it. But still I had a store of Soviet optimism in me, and I tried agonizingly to come to terms.

By spring of 1957, the novella was fininshed and my worst fears were immediately confirmed: Kataev flatly refused to print it. And you could understand him —the "thaw" of fifty-six was over. Completely different winds were blowing in literature. On every street corner they were thundering against the *Literary Moscow*[2] anthology and Dudintsev's novel *Not by Bread Alone*. Kataev certainly couldn't risk the magazine and his editing career over a young author's "libellous" novella. And just then Anatoly Kuznetsov's *Continuing Legend* came up. The beginning of it was great, just like real life, and boldy done—but such sniveling at the end![3] But it was precisely the end, the rebirth of the Komsomol legend, that the authorities liked best. That's the way to write, they told me.

But the sun doesn't rise and set on *Youth*. At the Soviet Writer Publishing House, they were getting "The Podgursky Chronicle" ready for publication. I took "The Brigantine" there. The publishing house efficiently produced two in-house reviews, in which I was accused of every possible ideo-political mistake. Honestly, after that I was really proud of myself—gee, what a dangerous book I wrote, it turns out...

There was anarchy at *New World*.[4] Simonov's team had left, Tvardovsky's hadn't come yet, and in the meantime Krivitsky was managing the show. He greeted me affectionately, and like an older comrade, he set me straight.

"As it is, the manuscript won't get through, it's too dreary."

I argued desperately, saying that everything in the book was just like real life. Krivitsky smiled indulgently.

"Marvelous. But you don't want the manuscript to rot in our desk here. Take my advice, I'm trying to help you. Go ahead, leave your favorite pages, but you've got to 'interleave' them with brighter episodes. Draw us a zebra—black stripe, bright stripe, black stripe, bright stripe... Step back—and you've got an objective picture."

He sincerely wished me well, and sent me off to Gorky[5] on business so that I could, first, get to know the working class better, and second, write another version of "The Brigantine."

By the Krivitsky episode, I wanted to show that it would be almost a sin for me to complain: as a rule, I've been lucky with editors. They were all interested in my books seeing the light of day and they all taught me how to write as you draw zebras—black stripe, bright stripe... Moreover, they were all sincerely convinced they were doing a good deed.

But even with sails painted like a zebra, "The Brigantine" wasn't launched right away. Inside, I was almost exultant: Krivitsky's formulas didn't work, meaning the book retained a lot of me, my innermost thoughts. However, as soon as the first liberal winds began to blow, "The Brigantine" sailed and sailed and even...

It started with an excerpt in *Komsomol Pravda*, then the newspaper *The Moscow Komsomol* published the book in its entirety, with sequels from issue to issue. And later the novella was reprinted in almost all the far eastern youth newspapers. The book was diligently translated in brotherly socialist countries. Was this an accident? Of course not. Clearly, the cunning Krivitsky had calculated accurately, and the friendly support of the official press was proof. I did not deceive the State, the State used me for its own ends.

The story of "The Brigantine" generally is very instructive. Before and after me, many writers have tried to beat the State at "who'll-outwit-whom?" We'll let them have one page if they give us the next. Who turned out ahead? Sometimes—the writers, but as a rule—the State. But most important, the State won the basic point: the writer was disposed to compromise beforehand. And compromise thinking led the writer to gradually retreat step by step. Thus arose a habit, which as we all know, is second nature—the habit of self-censorship. And suddenly, one fine day, it's clear that a supposedly "leftish" and honest author is a cosy literato tamed by the authorities.

Many have tried to outwit the State. We've played

these games with greater or less success. But to the honor of our generation, I would like to say that among us is one writer who from the first took no part in these "childish pastimes." He is Yury Kazakov, who published his first stories in 1957.

V

There aren't many geniuses in literature, but at the Gorky Literary Institute of the Writers' Union of the USSR, they have always been found in great numbers. Actually, you can figure there are as many geniuses as there are students—a hundred and fifty, I think. I studied for four years at the Lit Institute and can declare with complete confidence that even in the most specialized educational hothouse, it's impossible to raise a single writer artificially. Talent is still God's gift. However, in principle the Lit Institute was useful. It didn't at all hurt our homegrown genius poets and prosaists to become acquainted with the rudiments of history, geography, literary criticism, and to read a little Pushkin, Gogol, Dostoevsky and foreign classics together. Geniuses are an odd bunch—they're used to reading only themselves. But here, whether you wanted to or not, under threat of a "two" (a "D") on an exam[1] you had to open the textbook...

Nevertheless, you can excuse a lot in the students at the Lit Institute, because in most cases they were devotees. As a rule, the Lit Institute accepted persons around thirty years old. Overgrown students, who had already managed to raise families, gave up government or military careers, decent incomes and, tightening their belts, settled into a stipend—220 rubles in old money.[2] According to the most accurate accounting, such a stipend was just enough for only the most minimal grub plus bimonthly excursions to the baths (if you don't take soap[3]). But what can you do? Literature, as we all know, requires sacrifices.

Most of our attention was devoted, in any case, not to the lectures, but to the so-called creative seminars. There were ten or twelve students in each seminar. Leading the seminar was some venerable "classic," long forgotten by readers and publishers, and so, earnestly moonlighting in the field of education. But there were pleasant exceptions. During my time at the Lit Institute, Paustovsky, Svetlov, Arbuzov, Berezko, Zamoshkin taught there. Shklovsky, Bondi, and Bylinsky were visiting lecturers. But to return to the seminars, once a week the work of one of the students was discussed. That is, the hero of the day would read aloud some short story or narrative poem of his, and his friends and colleagues, "quietly and in a comradely manner," would analyze the merits and shortcomings of each opus in turn. In my opinion, discussion in the seminars was good practice for the future literati. In the creative atmosphere of "friendliness and comradeship" no one was shy, and they beat the birthday boy to a pulp, employing the most strongly prohibited methods. They beat him, of course, not in the literal sense. Although sometimes the creative discussion was transferred to Peredelkino, to the student dormitory, where it continued according to the ancient tit-for-tat principle.

I was discussed only twice, but even that tempering was enough for a long time. After the seminars at the Institute, even the roughest criticism from the press seemed mere tickling.

True, occasionally a student was praised to the skies. But then the tone was usually set by the seminar chairman, and the work fell into the category of "extremely solid ideologically." I remember I wandered into a senior course somehow and listened to just such a panegyric. I was surprised. But the chubby bald guy sitting next to me muttered gloomily through his teeth, "Do they really consider that good?"

That's how I met Yury Kazakov.

Kazakov gave the impression of a quiet, balanced, slightly ironic man who knew his own worth. In contrast to the rest of us, he entered literature a full-blown writer, and his first stories are just as good as his last.

Among the well-known prose writers who studied with me at the Lit Institute were Anatoly Kuznetsov, who had successfully made his debut in *Youth*, and Georgy Semenov, who, by the way, hadn't yet made an appearance then. Four of us in all—but that really isn't so few. There were more poets: Gennady Aigi, Vladimir Sokolov, Vladimir Tsybin... Robert Rozhdestvensky's star was rising; he was a good companion, an excellent athlete, captain of the Institute's volleyball team, a comedian—the life of the party. Who would imagine that in time our Robert would become Secretary of the Writers' Union of the USSR, and morosely, silently preside at solemn presidium meetings. Bella Akhmadulina was in the freshman class, then still a shy plump girl who astounded everyone with her poems, which bore the stamp of a great talent. But against this brilliant poetic background, one man stood out—Evgeny Alexandrovich Evtushenko. Students and teachers respectfully called him by name and patronymic,[4] and the numerous lit-institute geniuses at once fell silent if Evtushenko but appeared in the hall. Unlike with Rozhdestvensky, people behaved in various ways toward Evtushenko: they admired him, were exasperated by him, envied him... But they all talked about him. At one of the plenary sessions of the Writers' Union, when the defeat of the Moscow writers' "opposition" was complete, Evtushenko rose to the podium. Several of us students who had happened to make it into the hall were frozen in horror: "Why did Zhenya get up there? He'll disgrace himself; they'll tear him to pieces!" But Zhenya spoke with dignity, courage, he made the audience listen to him and concluded his speech with lines from Alexander Mezhirov, which sounded very significant:

> Party men con us our duty,
> The great Motherland loves us...
> The artillery's giving our own troops a thrashing,
> We're not making omelettes but we are
> > breaking eggs.

Nature was generous with Evtushenko! A brilliant poet and orator, how much he managed to accomplish later, both good and bad!

In general, I recall my first years at the Institute with affection. They coincided with an awakening of our society, with the Twentieth Party Congress,[5] with sharp polemics in literature. Actually, ideologically and spiritually, we took shape precisely in this period. But the short spring of liberalization was over, the State showed its claws, and in the Literary Institute, the situation changed drastically—the witch hunt had begun.

At meetings, they'd pick holes in "ideologically vicious" manuscripts. "Leftwingers" who didn't have a name in literature were expelled from the Institute. Well-wishers advised us to bite our tongues in seminars on the social sciences. Yury Kazakov's dissertation, that is, his published stories, was judged a "three" (satisfactory) by the credentials committee. Evtushenko and Akhmadulina also received their degrees "with high adventures..."

It is curious that this witch hunt within the Institute was conducted by dull, semi-literate students who hadn't shown in a creative sense, but were, on the other hand, activists; they did occupy important positions in the Party Committee, the Student Committee and the Komsomol Committee. Out of naiveté, I imagined that such union of talentlessness and aspiration to leadership was a purely lit-institute phenomenon. Alas, I was later convinced that such a picture is typical of the whole Union of Writers.

VI

In Moscow, on Mayakovsky Square, right above
the Sofia restaurant, are the offices of the editorial
board of a "literary and socio-political" magazine. The
visitor goes up to the third floor, rings the bell and, ac-
companied by the intent gaze of the porter, may stroll
about the spacious foyer and corridors. On the walls
hang paintings by young artists devoted to the great
building sites of communism. Here also are photographs of editorial staff taken during their speeches at
the oil fields at Tyumen.[1] The magazine sponsors the
Tyumen region, and for that reason—everywhere, charts
on petroleum output, fulfillment of the plan, construction of railways and pipelines. Perhaps it is not a literary
magazine, but a newspaper on socialist industry?...

In private offices the editors languish in boredom.
Revivification occurs only once a week, when they de-
liver the staff's food orders from the grocery store.[2]
The editor-in-chief is never on the premises. He's usually
abroad, but if he turns up in Moscow en route, he generally dines at the House of Writers with a delegation of
writers from Tanzania or Upper Volta. Nevertheless,
nothing disturbs the regular appearance of the magazine.
At the beginning of the month the colored covers of the
new issue show up in all the kiosks and gather dust
there until they're thrown in the same heap with the
preceding issues. What of it, a normal, successful Soviet

magazine, no better or worse than the others. Just take a look at the neon display by the entrance to the editorial offices, and your heart sinks—is this *Youth*? Militant, quarrelsome, loud-voiced *Youth* has come to this?

The first issue of the magazine came out in June 1956. Its circulation was respectable for the time—100,000. In five years its circulation had increased exactly five times. Why? They weren't printing stylish patterns for women's dresses or addictive crossword puzzles. Perhaps it was the special character of the youth theme? But *The Young Guard* magazine, also for young people, was being published simultaneously. So what, they barely managed to scrape together 60,000 readers. I speak from personal experience: you publish a story in *The Young Guard* and it's like yelling into an icehole—no echo. But get printed up in *Youth* and you set all the bells ringing. By 1965 the circulation of *Youth* had grown to one and a half million. Two years later—two million. True, there's nothing to read in it now, but the circulation remains the same, for in Russia inertia reigns.

The erratics of our literary criticism have developed in the reader an infallible scent: if the press praises some publication, no one will even pick it up, but if they rail against it on every street corner, that means the magazine's got something worthwhile. For a long time *New World* and *Youth* were running neck and neck, intermittently getting their teeth knocked in and their ears boxed with about equal frequency. But *New World* maintained a consistent literary level, while at *Youth* there were major slips. And then *New World* preserved its liberal tendency longer, while *Youth* more quickly yielded its position. But on the other hand, *New World* had a comparatively narrow circle of readers, basically the intelligentsia, while a whole generation grew up on

[43]

Youth. There were years when the official authorities forbade subscription to *Youth* in the army. That's how dangerous the magazine was declared to be! It had to earn that!

Several years ago my friends got the idea of writing a history of the Soviet liberal magazine. However, considering the Soviet censor, these plans were unrealistic. Now, one might think, Gladilin has the cards in his hands, let him go ahead and write... But, dear citizens, I declare quite frankly that there is no freedom of speech in the "accursed West" either. Just put yourself in my position: if I loudly damn some editorial scoundrel now, he'll get a promotion before you turn around; and if I praise a worthy man, he may be fired. What kind of freedom is that? But my task is made easier by the fact that with few exceptions there were neither open villains nor steadfast Don Quixotes on the editorial staff. The magazine employees themselves didn't know what they were doing. In our literature, it happens that in practice a man ends up a hero for no reason at all. But, as they say, not guilty by hide nor hair. Of course, in principle, the management of the magazine wasn't at all against doing good deeds if they didn't get beaten up for them. But since they did, and very badly at that, with the threat of getting fired, the management on the contrary tried desperately to "be vigilant," but alas...

The unenlightened reader no doubt thinks to this day that in better times *Youth* was done by secret counter-revolutionaries, undercover revisionists who dreamed of working sedition onto every page. Nothing of the kind! *Youth* was in the hands of old men who ran timorously from office to office and scared each other. "Oy, now we're in for it! Oy, the stuff we're printing! Oy, they'll lay into us right off!" What a jewel the permanent chief secretary alone was! A real workhorse, he came to the office earlier and left later than anyone else. He read each issue all the way through several times, to catch ideological mistakes, sniff out ambiguities.

In principle, every worker on the editorial staff was supposed to protect the interests of the magazine. But here's the typical picture. An issue has just been cleared by the censorship office. The chief secretary picks up the telephone and calls the censor himself: "Did you read it carefully? Didn't you find anything? Well—page seventeen, fifth line from the top, doesn't that passage bother you? No? It's permissible? And then—page fifty-five, eighth line from the bottom, doesn't that call up some associations? And the next paragraph down, I think that souds kind of strange..."

And so on. That's the sort of liberal who ran *Youth*. Nevertheless, they tried not to take offense at the chief secretary. In 1937 his wife was executed and he himself fled posthaste and escaped only by a miracle. Escaped, but was frightened for the rest of his life.

On occasion, the assistant editor would print a pointed article despite the editor-in-chief, because he wanted to prove that he, the assistant editor, wasn't low man on the editorial board.

However, when the critical wave fell and *Youth*'s management, catching its breath, realized that nothing terrible had happened, they all still had their jobs, and what's more, that the periodic pointed article only made the magazine more popular—the old men were sincerely happy and raised their glasses to the health of the seditious writer at the annual *Youth* banquet. By the way, those banquets were very gay; I attended more than once myself.

But of course the liberal tendency of the magazine

was preserved not because those old men missed something, and not even because of intrigues on the editorial staff. There was simply tremendous pressure from below. Young people greedily ate up every free word. It wasn't easy to withstand such pressure. They all felt it. That was the decisive factor.

...Liberal tendencies. Again one recalls the so-called "epoch of the liberalization of our lives." But why was this liberalization expressed largely in two magazines—*New World* and *Youth*—and for all practical purposes not even touching other literary publications? I don't think we would be talking about *New World* now if Simonov and later Tvardovsky hadn't been there. The same with *Youth*. There would have been no magazine (or rather, there would have been some superfluous provincial publication), if it hadn't been for Kataev.

Kataev held the position of editor-in-chief for about six years. But even in later years, Kataev's spirit was invisibly present on the editorial board. The new "chief"—Boris Polevoi—couldn't bring himself to betray Kataev's traditions immediately. What's more, to win popularity among progressive readers, Polevoi even tried to be bolder than Kataev. However, the Ideological Section of the Central Committee quickly called Polevoi to order and he hastened to reform.

Actually, Boris Nikolaevich Polevoi is a nice man, sociable, he could easily representationize (which he does, by the way) at the Foreign Commission of the Writers' Union, where during the evening meal (at state expense) one must convince the literati of Latin America or Black Africa of the advantages of socialist realism. No doubt Polevoi possesses other virtues as well, but for him, being editor-in-chief is categorically contra-indicated. But Kataev was not only born to be head of a magazine; in his every word, in his every comment in the margins of a manuscript, one perceived an important writer.

For a variety of reasons, I am not going to touch on Kataev's political views. In different periods of our socio-literary life he functioned differently. I know many respected people who have justifiable grievances with Kataev on that account. However, let us put the question differently: are there now in our literature any real, generally accepted master prosaists who have been able to preserve their sharp pen to this day? Indisputably, there are a few persons, but by right, Valentin Kataev heads this list. I shall take the liberty of remarking to Kataev's critics: first try living in a Soviet classic's skin awhile and then talk.

There are quite a few big names in Soviet literature. But basically they are authors of one or two good books. Later, these writers are either broken, and silent the rest of their days, or they are bought. It seems that the second possibility might apply to Kataev. In the twenties he loudly announced himself with his early stories and the play *Squaring of the Circle*, then wrote *White Shone the Lonely Sail* and later... And later came *Son of the Regiment, For Soviet Power* and the other official, made-to-order pieces. Who knows, probably Kataev would have remained a writer of untried potentials, the author of the classic *Sail* and editor-in-chief of a popular magazine for young people. But fate toys with man, as they say. Dismissed from his responsible position, Valentin Petrovich became seriously ill and was on the border of clinical death. That's apparently when he realized that it's actually very easy to die. And there's so much you have to get done. Then he stopped his wily game with the authorities and wrote three marvelous books one after the other: *The Holy Well, Grass of Oblivion, The Block*. In them he exposed himself utterly, in them he went beyond the frontier of the new "mauvist" prose.

What is "mauvism"? I shall not now explain seriously this term, which Kataev introduced into literature. I shall remark only that a definite stereotype had developed in Soviet prose writing. Kataev exploded these ossified forms and began to work in a free, independent manner. That isn't so insignificant a thing for our literature. It's practically revolutionary! We recall how many times writers have been beaten for formalism, modernism and other -isms. I repeat, some day, when there is a free literature in Russia, writers will be judged not only by what they wrote about but mainly *how* they wrote.

At that time it was strange to see Kataev in the position of disgraced literato. Kataev's *The Holy Well* wandered from magazine to magazine, and no one could bring themselves to publish the manuscript. And how could it be published when there's a Soviet diplomat at an official reception who washes his hands in the compote, a "talking cat" who dies without being able to pronounce the word "Vissarionovich,"[3] and a typical, most successful Soviet writer who is a "sturgeon puss, a man-agent by the name of Prokhindeikin" (the prototype, by the way, was Sergei Mikhalkov[4]). But the separate details aren't the point. As soon as Kataev's pen got a taste of freedom, it drew, most likely against the author's will, a really frightening picture of our life, which despite all the grotesque, was absolutely realistic... Perhaps I am mistaken, but it seems to me that if *The Holy Well* had appeared in the West first, it would have made no less of a stink than Boris Pasternak's *Doctor Zhivago*.

However, someone upstairs apparently figured you shouldn't lose "a living classic," on whose books more than one generation had been raised. *The Holy Well* was cleaned up and passed. And after three "mauvist" books, Kataev himself settled down a bit and went back to the old rut... Nevertheless, here's what's curious: when Kataev, back in the bosom of the motherland, was given the title Hero of Socialist Labor, not a word was spoken, in all the articles devoted to this significant event, of his best prose: *The Holy Well, Grass of Oblivion, The Block*. As if these books didn't exist! That's the sort of wonders that occur in "the most advanced and progressive" literature of the world.

I took the liberty of speaking a bit more in detail of Valentin Petrovich Kataev because I wish to show by his example that a great talent always will out. No matter what blinders the writer puts on himself, no matter how tightly "the only correct ideology" binds his hands —eventually the time will come when the living word will break through. But while Kataev was editor-in-chief of *Youth*, his new literary style was perceptible not in his own work, but in the writings of those young authors whom Kataev first published in his magazine. Kataev sort of tested himself on others.

VII

It was remarked long ago that, recalling events from the past, man unwittingly embellishes them. Thus even in Solzhenitsyn, former prisoners of the "Archipelago" speak of the years of confinement behind barbed wire with trembling emotion... And when the conversation comes around to my success among the reading public—how can I not shed a tear of emotion! However, let's get a handkerchief, wipe up and try to tell how it was in fact. To begin, let's give the floor to Valentin Kataev. In the magazine's anniversary issue, Number 6 for 1975 (*Youth* was then celebrating its twentieth year), Kataev wrote that at first the magazine just wasn't able to win popularity. They happened to print Thor Heyerdahl's *Kon-Tiki*, and *Youth*'s modest circulation jumped. Encouraged by success, Kataev commissioned a translation of Hemingway's novella *The Old Man and the Sea*. But then the most extraordinary thing occurred (I quote Kataev):

> ...Into my office, with a fox's tread and a dissembling smile on his lips, between which smoked a fetid cigar, walked the editor of one of our fraternal magazines and, taking me aside, whispered conspiratorially, "Don't do it, I beg of you! I've just been, so to speak, in certain circles... With one young man, I won't give his

name... You understand... hmmm... And he—but this is strictly between us—spoke very unfavorably of Hemingway's work as a whole and of *The Old Man and the Sea* in particular. He called Papa Hem...a 'half-baked decadent' and *The Old Man and the Sea* 'dangerous petty-bourgeois nonsense'..."

I went pale, because I knew that my benevolent brother-editor of our fraternal magazine was constantly weaving around in those circles and it was dangerous to ignore his advice.

That's exactly how they advised Kataev out of printing Saint-Exupery's *Le Petit Prince*. I continue the quotation:

"Enough!" I cried mentally, and when, soon after, manuscripts by Anatoly Gladilin, Vasily Aksenov and several remarkable young poets arrived at the editorial offices, I firmly decided not to yield, despite the evil drone of the various "friends" of our young magazine. I messed up on Hemingway, I messed up on Saint-Exupery, but I will stick up for our native Russian geniuses. I printed them. To everyone's surprise, it came off. New names were up in lights and *Youth*'s circulation crept upward, like the temperature of a flu-ridden invalid, yet it didn't come to pneumonia, and we got off with a minor scare.

As we can see, the former editor-in-chief of *Youth* had his difficulties, and not inconsiderable ones. But what's curious is that for *Youth*'s current editor-in-chief, life proves even more difficult. It turned out that he wasn't supposed to print these "Memoirs" of Kataev's. One wonders what is so terrible in them? Uh-uh! The man who once walked into Kataev's office "with a fox's tread, smoking a fetid cigar" recognized his portrait and became terribly upset. And since this man is none other than the now powerful editor of *The Literary Gazette*, Alexander Chakovsky, there was a fantastic scandal. Kataev—Soviet "classic," Hero of Socialist Labor—was forced, like a little boy, to write an explanatory memorandum to the Central Committee. The editorial staff of *Youth* timorously made excuses. They put on a whole show. Boris Polevoi maintained that he hadn't read the anniversary issue of the magazine at all (?!). The prudent permanent chief secretary presented his own alibi: he was on vacation at the time, so he says. In the end, the assistant editor Yury Voronov was burned out—they simply fired him. "O tempore! O mores!" Before, you got off with a minor scare for taking a few liberties, now organizational cutbacks are required.

But let's get back to Kataev's memoirs. As I said, Kataev published my "Chronicle of the Times of Viktor Podgursky" in 1956, but absolutely refused to print "The Brigantine." He didn't want to print a few of my stories either, so the path of those whom Kataev called "young Russian geniuses" wasn't exactly strewn with roses. However, I personally don't bear Valentin Petrovich any grudges. The editor-in-chief of *Youth* had to avoid taking sides. Taking the current state of affairs into account, Kataev ran the magazine on the principle: let them run gray, jingoistic stories for a year, but in one issue there's got to be a sharp "scandal" piece. And it was precisely thanks to one of those publications that *Youth*'s circulation rose so fabulously. In 1957, Kataev printed Anatoly Kuznetsov's *Continuing Legend*.

In 1959, Vasily Aksenov came to the magazine and brought two stories—God knows what they were like, but Kataev truly recognized the "future genius" in the young author. He persuaded Aksenov to write a novel about doctors—and so *Colleagues* appeared, making the young writer a national celebrity.

As for me, I too received Kataev's official recognition only in 1959. My new novella *Smoke in Your Eyes*, a piece which is still dear to me, was lying around in the editorial office. I am convinced that it's of interest even now, if only for its formal innovations. But the magazine staff, apparently used to my so-called failures after "The Chronicle," treated the manuscript coolly. Soon it became known that Kataev didn't like *Smoke in Your Eyes* either. Nevertheless, he called me in for a chat, warning me that the conversation would be of a purely formal character.

"You have a right to your opinion, and I to mine," Kataev announced bluntly. "Your manuscript is too complicated and incomprehensible in its structure. Now if you wrote a little tale of say twenty pages on this material..."

I had practically no chance of pushing *Smoke in Your Eyes* through, but I didn't give up.

"But why is the novella complicated and incomprehensible?" I asked Kataev. "In *Time Forward* you even put the first chapter all the way at the end."

Kataev's eyes flared up, and he explained the structure of his novel to me in detail, even sketched a diagram on a sheet of paper. Then I in turn sketched the composition of *Smoke in Your Eyes*. And then a miracle occurred. Valentin Kataev scratched the top of his head and drawled, "Perhaps you're right. Well, all right, we'll chance printing it."

And the novel was printed in the magazine, though

[53]

with some incidents, it's true. First, the censor pulled it from the issue, crossing out things from the proofs with different colored pencils, like an abstract painting. Then, three months later, the same censor signed the novella through to publication almost without objections. The logic of censors is incomprehensible to me to this day. But that's not the main thing. In my opinion, it's a rare event when a simple Soviet author can convince the editor-in-chief to accept a manuscript towards which the chief was already negatively disposed. I was always a dreadful speaker, so it wasn't my doing. It's simply that this time, Kataev's editorial sense came into play. And such breadth of vision isn't met with often in our literature.

VIII

Telling of my literary affairs, I've jumped ahead a bit. Let's return to April 1958, when one fine day I crossed the threshold of the literature and art department of the newspaper *The Komsomol Muscovite*. There were about ten people sitting in the room—staff members, authors, poets from the lit association. They looked at me without curiosity—clear enough, here comes another "teapot" (that's what editorial staffers called graphomaniacs). For some reason I was very nervous and started talking, confusedly and at length, so no one understood a thing. Finally they asked me condescendingly, "You bring some poems?"

I gave my name. Their faces fell. Only then did they all understand that the new boss had arrived.

...How truly the ancient authors showed, "Strange are the ways of the Lord!" Just two months before, I had passed the early exams for the fourth-year course at the Lit Institute and transferred to the correspondence section. Why? The witch hunt at the Lit Institute had reached such a pitch that I decided I had to take off for good and all. Through the Ministry of the Navy I intended to get fixed up as a sailor on an ocean-going ship (naturally, with calls in foreign ports). I wanted to know a different sort of life, I wanted to see a little of other countries, in sum, the "romance of the road" called me. But that's when the Komsomol organization of the Lit Institute found a way to settle accounts with me. They gave me such recommendations that I'd be lucky to get a job as a night watchman, much less overseas travel.

And suddenly...they called me and offered me the position of department head at the newspaper. If later, during the flowering of my literary career, I'd been unexpectedly named minister of culture, it wouldn't have seemed as incredible a flight as that moment. From undergraduate to administrator! And then, according to the *nomenklatura*[1] I was now ranked as Secretary of the Komsomol Regional Committee. Fantastic!

However, this was scarcely some permanent staffer's whimsy. It was a deliberate policy of advancement of the young cadres. They were buying me. It was implied that "inspired by the Party's trust," I would work as one ought. And I really tried...

This episode clearly shows by what principle people were selected to control the literary, artistic and theatrical life of Moscow. Of course, I was then very little suited for this position from the professional point of view. Only one thing reassured me: my editorial staff had even less understanding of literature and art than I.

For the sake of objectivity I should mention that I still wasn't confirmed as department head. The area committee secretary didn't like me. Why? Perhaps the shrewd secretary discerned my incompetence? No, the secretary shrewdly discerned that I was wearing tight pants. "What a *stilyaga* you've got over there!" the secretary said to the editor-in-chief of the newspaper. And for more than a year I worked happily as acting department head.

But then I developed a quite proper relationship with another administrator, Secretary of the City Committee on Propaganda Yury Verchenko. Verchenko would invite me to his office at the City Committee, and then there would be a conversation something like this:

"Tolya, have you seen such-and-such a performance? What's your opinion?"

I gave my honest opinion.

"And how did you like such-and-such a film?"

I gave an oral review.

"And what do you think about this book?"

I explained in detail what I thought of it.

At first I imagined that Yury Verchenko was simply an "interested comrade," and he needed these chats to see general trends. But once I chanced to hear one of his reports on some film: the Secretary of the City Committee repeated in detail, word for word, my analysis, and then added his Party-spirited, ideological conclusions. During the break, a well-known film buff, who'd also been invited to this meeting, told me, "What a cultured man that secretary of yours is, he knows all about..."

I smiled and thought, so that's what it means to make good use of the cadres. By the way, that style secured Verchenko a rapid rise: he transferred to the Central Committee of the Komsomol, then to the Party City Committee, and now he's a b-i-i-i-g man—Organizational Secretary of the Union of Writers of the USSR. In practice, he runs the whole show at the union.

It's rather interesting to trace the "directives" the administration has handed us. There were, of course, some sharp turnabouts, when the editor-in-chief would run in foaming from the regional committee and shout from the doorway, "Not another word about the old Bolsheviks!" or "Not a single positive item on China!"

But I mean editorial policy in questions of literature and art. For example, the management is extremely reluctant to include an ordinary review in an issue, but always very enthusiastic about a critical rout or a blow-up. (This is called—the newspaper taking a hard line.) Once we really lit into the Shchepkin Drama School, and Vera Nikolaevna Pashennaya, a National Actress of the USSR,[2] was forced to come to our department and persuade, beg us to make a retraction. What was she supposed to do? After all, an article in the newspaper, even if it was written by some girl-journalist, is not merely the voice of the public so much as a very unambiguous appeal for organizational cutbacks at the Moscow Theater Administration.

Naturally, the editor-in-chief preferred publishing literary stories on production themes. Usually a story was greeted simply with the question, "What's it about?" When the department was preparing a feature page on the poets and poetry of a factory literary association, the editor-in-chief cackled like a grouse in heat. When we tried to get a little collection of love poems through, the boss made a sour face. In this regard, the only exception was Devetyarov, assistant editor of *Komsomol Pravda*, where I worked later on. Every time poems were placed on his desk, he'd read through them slowly, fall into reverie, and utter the same phrase, "I don't understand." Well, how can you explain poetry to a man who doesn't understand it? Not for your life! But you had to explain it, for nothing got in the issue without the boss' pass.

IX

I hope I haven't reached the age where I have to write memoirs already. Recounting individual episodes from my life, I wish to evoke the atmosphere in which my generation grew up. A great many of my literary colleagues have gone through the school of Komsomol newspapers and magazines. And personally I recall *The Moscow Komsomol* with great warmth. I liked working on the newspaper. Of course, there were all sorts of people there, but the guys who were honestly trying to do a good job stood out. More liberties were taken in the city Komsomol newspaper, since the opinion of *The Moscow Komsomol* wasn't perceived as an approved directive from above anyway. The journalists received small salaries, fees in general were miserly, but the young people worked enthusiastically, stayed late at the office, fought for position on the page—naturally, it was an opportunity to have your say. Later on, when I ended up at *Komsomol Pravda*, I often compared the lively, seething milieu of *The Moscow Komsomol* with the academic calm of a large newspaper. At the *Komsomol* there was just no room for spontaneous action. Every word had to be approved by the Komsomol Central Committee. But if you go down from the sixth floor, which the *Komsomol* occupies, you immediately get the feeling you've landed in a crematorium. The deserted, dead corridors of the *Pravda* central office, where each lit worker has his own office, and it's completely incomprehensible what he does there. You see, a lit worker at *Pravda* comes out with a tiny paragraph twice a year maximum in his newspaper. In our journalism, there is a paradoxical situation. For example, a talented young fellow is transferred from the regional Komsomol newspaper to *Komsomol Pravda*. It would seem like a promotion. But the journalist no longer feels his former, if relative, freedom, and writes more rarely and worse. And when he's transferred even higher, to the *Pravda* central office, everyone knows you can give this journalist up for lost. But then, the work's not tough and the salary's gigantic.

At *The Moscow Komsomol*, my battle with the management proceeded with varying success. Let's assume I managed to print a satirical article on MKhAT[1] (apparently, the first during the whole existence of the Soviet state). I didn't like MKhAT's nonsense about contemporary youth, but the management didn't catch on to what I was doing, though they did like the sharp tone of the article. True, when the pillars of theatrical society got upset, the editor-in-chief tore out his hair...

We almost never did jingoistic holiday poems— we proved to the editorial board that in principle they are all potboilers. But on the other hand, when a dirty, libellous article on the ASCI[2] was brought to the paper and our department came out against it, the editor-in-chief didn't take our opinion into account and printed the article in the department on Komsomol life.

However, despite everything, you'd like to remember the good, so I'll tell the story of a Soviet Cinderella, a story I myself participated in.

It was a frosty winter day. We're in the staff car, like Pinkertons wandering around Bolshevsky region in the Moscow area. At last we find the building we want. An old, half-ruined barrack. With difficulty we squeeze into a small room with a tiny window. In the half-gloom we make out heaps of rags, mattresses, blankets, on which .sat a young girl with a sickly, emphysematose face. There wasn't a single chair in the room. Infernal cold. The girl was obviously frightened by our arrival.

"Are you Novella Matveeva?"

"Yes," the girl answered timidly.

"Come with us, we're from *Komsomol Pravda*."

We just barely got Matveeva to the editorial office —she couldn't stand riding in a car. The employees gasped when they saw what terrible rags Matveeva was wearing. The women pooled together and bought her some necessary things. Novella Matveeva lived a week in the *Komsomol Pravda* hotel, while the literature and art department of the newspaper selected and edited her poems. A whole page of Novella Matveeva's poems appeared, and thus a well-known Soviet poetess was born.

Later on the press coyly wrote that Novella Matveeva, "girl of the people," worked as a herdswoman(!). In fact, she was a domestic servant in an officer's family; she managed to complete only one year of primary school, and only thanks to books and her mother's help could she study independently. The fee *Komsomol Pravda* wrote out seemed an unheard-of fortune to Matveeva. Soon Novella Matveeva was accepted into the Union of Writers, and as far as I know, her career turned out happily every after.

However, in order for this miracle to occur, an incredible confluence of fortunate circumstances was required. The poems of the then completely unknown poetess, which were gathering dust in the editorial offices of the area Komsomol newspapers (Matveeva sent them out regularly, and was not even favored with a reply), accidentally fell into the hands of a good poet. The poet accidentally brought them to the Komsomol

Central Committee. Just at that time, Len Karpinsky was named third secretary of the Komsomol Central Committee—a completely accidental appointment in that bureaucratic organization. Len Karpinsky wanted to present a new style of work and didn't brush the poems aside (as any of his predecessors would have done), but called *Komsomol Pravda* to find the girl. There are thousands of Matveevs in Moscow area, and we never would have found her, but the rare name Novella helped.

The careers of honest Komsomol journalists of my generation didn't turn out as happily as Matveeva's. True, some of them reached executive positions, but they quickly "got their necks broken." They got one for a pointed article, another for the independent line of his newspaper, a third was never forgiven for refusing to publish the appropriate material during our troops' invasion of Czechoslovakia. Talented fellows without exception, and all of that pleiad are now in third-rate posts. The only ones whose careers were successful were the gray little spineless officials who always kept their noses to the wind. As for Len Karpinsky (adopted son of the old Bolshevik Karpinsky), despite his brilliant prospects, he didn't get along in the system. The system demands obedience and submission and does not tolerate black sheep. Karpinsky was subsequently lowered in rank; he didn't even stay in the *nomen-klatura*. A year ago, Karpinsky was expelled from the Party and sacked.

X

The line from *Eugene Onegin*—"A restlessness took hold of him, desire for a change of scene."[1] —could be applied to our whole generation. As a rule, first, books appeared as a result of work somewhere in the sticks or endless travels in remote regions of the country. The young literati sailed on seiners, flew to the North Pole, marched with geological expeditions... Moreover, if these were road assignments from magazines, the fellows didn't boast of the fact that they were journalists, but tried to "learn life" up close. For example, Anatoly Kuznetsov worked at the Bratsk HES[2] as a concrete worker, Viktor Konetsky sailed the Arctic Ocean as a navigator, Georgy Vladimov "trucked" at the Kursk metallurgical complex... However, I think that the desire for a change of scene was not only a result of the romance of the road characteristic of youth. We were Soviets, we believed the newspapers. The newspapers threw in over and over that at the great constructions sites, in the tundra and taiga, real life was in full swing. For some reason we could not discover that elusive "real life" in Moscow or Leningrad and sought it in the boundless expanses of the Union.

By the spring of 1959, I should have been confirmed in the position of head of the literature and art department of *The Moscow Komsomol* newspaper. For this, there was but one requirement: join the Party.

I was satisfied with my job—go to theaters, see new films, mix with the creative intelligentsia—what more could I dream of, really? Work in the department was going well, I could quietly continue the administrative-journalistic career I'd so successfully begun, especially since at *Youth* Kataev finally accepted my new novella *Smoke in Your Eyes.*

And then I was seized by that cursed restlessness. It ended with me leaving the paper and flying off to Magadan on a road assignment for *The Young Guard* magazine.

"On the road rose Magadan, capital of Kolyma..."—a line from a well-known prison-camp song.[3] Kolyma, wrapped in ominous mystery, is the place millions of political prisoners perished.

"Cursed be thou, Kolyma, called a wonder of the planet, you'll lose your mind if you will or no, from here there's no return..."—words from the same song. But I repeat, I flew to Magadan in May 1959; I was authoritatively assured that there were no longer any camps left in Kolyma and even shown the site of a former camp—ruined barracks, torn barbed wire... And in general the journalist from Moscow was received "on a high level."

However, conversations in administrative offices didn't satisfy me. I was full of "Komsomol fervor" and firmly intended to "learn life up close." In the *sovnarkhoz*[4] (we still had *sovnarkhozes* then) my request was handled with understanding and I was assigned to a gold mine—naturally, the very best, a model mine where Komsomol volunteers worked with recruited workers. The mine was even named "The Komsomol" and was located in Chukotka,[5] a mere thousand kilometers from Magadan—for our North, that's no distance at all. I hoped that I would be absolutely incognito at the mine, but for some reason the mine management in turn assigned me to the best, the leading crew.

I shall not poetize our exploits on the labor front, although my name appeared by chance among the production leaders in the regional newspaper. But I know that I just barely coped with the work. The day shift lasted twelve hours, then twenty-four hours rest, then twelve hours on the night shift. And so on with no days off or holidays. By the time you drag yourself from the work zone to the settlement, by the time you wash up, eat supper, get your sleep—you just turn around and your rest is over, and it's time to get back to the diggers again. Before the gold mines, I considered myself a pretty strong guy, but here I was obviously inferior to my mates. In short, I very quickly ran off to an easier position—as a blacksmith's striker. By the way, the money I earned was enough for me to fly from Chukotka to Kamchatka and from there to Vladivostok and Khabarovsk.

At the gold mines, it wasn't the Komsomol volunteers who made the strongest impression on me (though we'll get back to them later), but the "recruits," that is, workers long ago recruited for the North, with rather checkered backgrounds. Here's how one of the characters in my novella *Songs of the Gold Mines* tells of himself:

> I hacked mica near Tobolsk and nearly starved my ass off prospecting. And I did the Okhotsk sea route, knifed a guy in Yagodny, took a MAZ[6] out to Osumkchan, drank cologne on the Southern, swore at the meetings in Kaatyr. I borrowed Vaska's last fiver in Pevek and spent ten thousand in booze on the Vladivostok Express. I had five broads in Khabarovsk.

[65]

I saw the Pacific, swam in Baikal, went after a bear in Primore, and ate omul as slippery as soap in Chukchis' *yarangas*.[7] I been through so much, brother, you'd never dream. I've got a thick skin. You just can't get at me. But... You think, brother—I don't know—that I'm thirty and don't got house or home and only the lower bunk in a trailer, a watch and a couple of suits in a bag. ... But you know, brother, out near Kursk, in a little house with a half fallen-in roof and the windowframes starting to rot a little, my old mom's waiting for me, and I haven't brought her nothing but trouble and easy money. But I'm all she's got. I sent her a warm shawl and didn't write a single letter...

That's the sort of character. Of course, sitting in Moscow, you wouldn't think up one like that.

An interesting detail: the living prototype of my hero claimed in his monologue that he had a wife in Gorky and ten broads in Khabarovsk. That's how it was in my manuscript. But when the novella went to the censor's office (of course, I didn't know whether on his own initiative or after consulting upstairs) the censor crossed out "a wife in Gorky" and replaced "ten broads" with "five." From this I understood that apparently it is permissible for a single Soviet man to have five broads (sans wife)...

[66]

There was a certain playwright named Surov, a
Stalin Prize laureate,[1] author of Stalin's favorite play,
Green Street. After 1956, Surov was expelled from
the Union of Writers, since it turned out that all of
Surov's plays had been written by other persons, so
called "literary niggers." The former well-known playwright was then very humbly vegetating as a permanent
staffer of the Radio Committee, but naturally dreamed
of rising and becoming famous again. Once he met a
good crew of railway workers from the Moscow-Sortiro-
vochnaya station. Surov persuaded them to become a
"Communist labor brigade," that is, announce publicly
that henceforth they would work and live in a Communist manner. The fellows were simple, credulous,
and they couldn't have cared less what their crew
was called. But Surov's initiative was not supported
by the Radio Committee: "What difference does it
make what kind of stuff they think up?" muttered
the boss. "They got no instructions like that!" Half a
year passed, and Adzhubei, editor-in-chief of *Komsomol Pravda,* chanced to hear of this as-yet-unknown
brigade. Unlike the clumsy Radio Committee boss,
Adzhubei quickly grasped what sort of propagandistic
effect a new "workers' initiative" could have. Practically
the whole *Komsomol* rushed out to Moscow-Sortiro-
vochnaya Railway Station, and two days later the whole

paper was devoted to this "Communist brigade." After the paper came out, a sensational campaign started in the whole Soviet press. "Communist brigades" were organized by directive in every enterprise. Every day on the radio, they played the cheerful song:

> We're heading for Communism
> In the Communist brigade...

When I was getting ready to go to Magadan, the "Communist brigade" movement was in full swing. And of course, since I landed in the "Communist brigade" of the most advanced mine in Chukotka, I attempted to understand the essence of this movement.

In my novella *Songs of the Gold Mine,* Verkhov, a member of the Communist brigade, conveys his sense of the production process this way:

> When you rake the shovel under the bunker, all bent up, when the mud runs in little streams down your collar, when instead of pulling out a shovelful, you can't pull the shovel out, or make a sharp move and hit your hand or forehead against an iron upright, when the bunker of digger four is set up so half-assed it puts almost as much dirt on the belt as under the tray, and for hours and hours, almost without a breather you've got to throw thick, heavy mud first out to the edge of the pit and then onto the transport belt—then you understand that this is the end of the world they've got set up here.

The real prototype for Verkhov then added that he

dreams of meeting the author of the songs about the Communist brigades:

> It's really something to think up words like that
> "Week-day work-days are holidays for us..."
> I'd just like to see the shit-head for a minute,
> just get my hands on his ass!"

Of course I couldn't include Verkhov's last monologue in the story.

Among the Komsomol volunteers at the gold mine there were many marvelous fellows, but they didn't come there to break production records—they came for the good pay. The mine management gave the Communist brigades the work areas with greater gold deposits. Of course, you could earn more there, and so the fellows rushed into the combrigades. In each trailer, that is, little moveable wooden houses, the workers lived what's called "out of a common pot." There's no other way with the conditions in the North. But in the language of the management, such elementary communal life was called a "struggle for the communist way of life." True, some of the Komsomol activists hoped that they'd manage to get the mine in their own hands and make the management meet the needs of the workers a little more expeditiously. However, the autonomous rule of the Komsomol Committee didn't last long. Jigging season brought chronic production and supply deficiencies. Bulldozers broke down, there wasn't enough pipe, the pumps were out of order, the diggers' motors were rusted (once they got motors for the mine, they threw them right out in the snow, and let them lie there all winter—it would have been odd if they hadn't rusted). There were collosal lines at the cafeteria. At the store, you couldn't buy workshirts, T-shirts or shorts. And most important—they withheld wages.

To the workers' just demands, the management replied demagogically: "Are you afraid of a few difficulties? Was it any easier at Perekop or at Magnitogorsk?[2] Was it any easier for Sasha Matrosov when he marched against fascist machine-guns? When the nation is straining every nerve to meet the seven-year plan ahead of schedule, and make yet another step toward Communism, the members of the Communist labor brigade discuss T-shirts and shorts!"

And so on...

That is, the standard situation, characteristic of all the "great construction sites," repeated itself at the model Komsomol mine—the management wanted to compensate for errors in planning and supply deficiencies with the enthusiasm of the masses. That's what I wrote about in my novella.

I returned to Moscow, worked a short time at *Komsomol Pravda,* and then I was accepted into the Union of Writers. *Songs of the Gold Mine* was published in the June 1960 issue of *The Young Guard* magazine. The newspaper *Literature and Life* gave the novella a favorable review, but this was soon followed by a resolution from the Magadan Party Regional Committee, in which I was accused of libel. The Komsomol Central Committee also adopted an appropriate statement. The *Komsomol Pravda* critic, my former colleague, called me at home one night and informed me in a muffled whisper that he'd been forced to write a devastating article on my novella.

Elkin's article in the *Komsomol* was called "Of What Does the Anvil Sing?" The author declared that "it is difficult to think of a greater profanation of the very bases of the Communist labor brigade then 'the

Mikhailovite movement' portrayed in the novella *Songs of the Gold Mine...* In Anatoly Gladilin's writer's forge it was not the sun of our life that shone, but a distorted mirror image of it, and the sparks flying from the anvil—those splinters of a distorting mirror— did not light the people's way, but injured their souls."

Komsomol and Party magazines responded to the article in the *Komsomol.* Apparently a directive was given on my account, and I wasn't printed anywhere for two years. I don't deny that, personally, I was hurt, because the second wave of liberalization had begun, and writers of my generation entered literature "on a wide victorious front."

XII

Here I would like to make a slight digression. I would be unfair to enumerate only the bumps and bruises I was afforded by the critics.

I have already mentioned that I was accepted into the Union of Writers (January 21, 1960). I was the youngest member of that organization. In the Moscow branch of the Union of Writers, they treated me all right, and even more—sometimes I felt I was in the position of "favorite" (apparently my youth and directness impressed many). I was elected to the prose section office, and then there was talk that I'd be allowed... No, incredible! I didn't believe it till the very last minute.

And then that unimaginably happy day arrived when I descended the airplane ramp at Le Bourget airport and a charming Frenchwoman, a customs employee cursorily looked through my "hammer-and-sickled" passport,[1] smiled sweetly at me, and in answer I... I was feverishly trying to recall how I should answer. My entire vocabulary in French, which I'd studied for ten years, escaped me, and so, finding nothing appropriate, I said with some strange accent, "Spasibó, bolshoé!"[2]

So in March 1961 I was in Paris, I arrived as part of a tourist group of Moscow writers, including such well-known literati as Vsevolod Ivanov, Veniamin

Kaverin, Yury Bondarev, Grigory Baklanov, Alexander Gladkov, Leonid Zorin, Wilhelm Levick. It was one of the first group trips for writers abroad. These weren't secretaries of the Union of Writers, or lit-bureaucrats with appropriate errands, but simply writers. And most likely everything that was going on seemed a miracle not only to me, but to my older companions. Two weeks in France lay before us—seven days in Paris, seven days in the south of France. And of course, a trip along the Riviera was wonderful too, but if I'd had my way, I wouldn't have left Paris for a moment.

Naturally, we visited the Louvre, the Museum of the Impressionists, the Museum of Modern Art, the Rodin Museum, the editorial offices of *L'Humanite,* Notre Dame Cathedral—and it was all very interesting, but personally, just walks along the streets of Paris afforded me the greatest pleasure. The city was flooded with spring sunshine. I could have wandered endlessly along the boulevards and lanes, looking at the shop windows and the outdoor cafés, at the flocks of pretty girls in mini-skirts, admiring every building in Paris, every one... Monmartre, Montparnasse, le boulevard Italien... You wanted to pinch yourself—are you dreaming all this, are you really in Paris?

In a Parisian crowd, our delegation of writers probably looked like a group of displaced refugees from the war. In long trenchcoats and dark hats we moved in close ranks, and for some reason we all held our hands behind our backs.

"How do they know we're Russians?" Grigory Baklanov asked me.

I looked him over from head to foot and burst out laughing.

"Grisha, your cap is the only one like it in Paris, there isn't another in the whole city."

We had a tall, beautiful, energetic woman assigned to us as Intourist guide, Inna Yurievna. I thought she was going to perform the functions of a normal translator, but to my surprise I soon learned that she was virtually the director of our delegation, and what a director! On the tour bus she counted heads as if we were chicks and loudly ordered, "Don't get out! Don't talk! Don't lag!" and the respected writers would submit obediently and only call her Else Koch behind her back.

Once, during our trip in the south of France, she wouldn't let us off the bus at all. In return we composed a *chastushka*[3] (I've substituted decent words for the indecent ones):

> Having shown my *discipline,* which Inna Yurievna
> can *keep,*
> Today I'm going off to Nîmes with neither *food*
> nor *sleep.*

The *chastushka* is called "Greetings from Arles."

Students from the Russian department at Aix were waiting for us; they wanted to socialize with some Soviet writers. A crowd of young people were standing by the road. We were quite ready for any sort of conversation, but Inna Yurievna had decided differently for us: "Don't get out! There might be questions from provocateurs!" The tour bus braked to a halt, and leaning out of the window, Inna Yurievna quickly explained to the students that we were late. I yelled out, "Aren't you ashamed in front of the kids!"—But no one backed me up. The writers sat there with their heads hanging. The students followed us with sympathetic looks.

All in all, during our trip in the south, the beauties of France ceased to exist for me. All of my strength was spent in the vague struggle with our guide-director. In Marseilles I openly started a row with Inna Yurievna and went off to the movies in the company of a fellow from the Franco-Soviet Friendship Organization. That same evening I was worked over at the group meeting. I just couldn't understand what I'd done wrong. After all, my companion was a Frenchman from an organization friendly to us.

"He's a spy; he wanted to provoke you!" they repeated in chorus.

How, in what way?

(By the way, later on we got to be friends with this "spy." He joined the Party, came to Moscow and worked at Progress Publishers for several years, translating Lenin.)

Most likely I unfairly accused our guide-director of every sin. There was one area where she sincerely tried to help us—when it came to shopping trips. Each of us possessed the enormous sum of 120 francs.[4] If we wanted simply to take a stroll or visit a museum not in the plan, Inna Yurievna would start getting nervous and tried to dissuade us in every possible way. "Why?" she'd say, "What for?" But as soon as someone decided to buy something, the guide's eyes lit up. She could understand an interest in clothes. And I don't deny, she gave practical advice.

But I didn't come here for clothes! I dreamed of simply wandering through the streets of Paris.

Simply wander... Far from it! In accordance with our instructions, we had the right to walk in groups of no less than four persons, indicating our precise itinerary and under no circumstances consorting with people who addressed us in Russian. One fine day I discovered that our writers were ostracizing me, and no one would ask me to a foursome for a stroll.

"Grisha, Yura!" I cried, offended, to Bondarev and

Baklanov. "Don't you be sons of bitches too, take me with you!"

"Tolya," Bondarev whispered, looking around uneasily, "we'd like to, but you understand, if you come with us, you're sure to have a tail on you—either Inna Yurievna or that chap..."

"What chap?" I said, amazed.

"Why, the one they always put in your room."

Indeed, there was a journalist in our group who was completely unknown to me, such a modest, quiet young man. So that's where he's from. Everything's clear. And it's not worth getting upset with the fellows. It would be sort of inconvenient for them, former frontline officers, to march in a convoy too.

They all went off, and of the writers only I was left behind in the hotel lobby. To my right sits Inna Yurievna, to my left—the bashful chap. The Paris streets are flooded with spring sunshine, the cafés are open, the girls are strolling, and I have but one desire— to send them all to hell and fly back to Moscow today! I can't take it anymore!

"Tolya," Inna Yurievna suggests sympathetically, "maybe we could drop into the Galerie LaFayette?"

To a store again? No! I stand up and walk out of the hotel. Inna Yurievna and the "journalist" follow me. I walk several blocks, turn around—and my fellow travelers' faces are dripping with sweat. So much the better. I speed up. In Moscow, my friends joked that I could outdistance a trolley.

"Tolya," comes the suppressed cry behind me, "where are you headed?"

"Montparnasse, boulevard Saint-Michel, Lyons Station..."

"But that's half of Paris, and in two hours we have supper..."

"At my pace, I'll make it."

They believe me—I really will make it, but what'll they do? A minute's conference, and my bodyguards give up.

"OK, Tolya, don't be late. Just in case, here's the Embassy telephone, the consulate telephone, the military attaché's telephone and our telephone numbers at the hotel."

So I won two hours of freedom. And for two hours I walked along through the streets of Paris, which I dreamed of later in Moscow every night for two years.

They didn't let me go abroad again...

XIII

... Sometimes it seems even to me that this is all "the tales of ages long since past, the lore of deep antiquity."[1] Often, when I recall events fifteen years back, I notice a certain irritation and irony in the eyes of my interlocutors—as if to say, enough fabricating, we're tired of these tales from Weighty Wood. But they aren't fabrications or tall tales. It all happened.

... There was a huge crowd around the Polytechnical Museum. People asked for extra tickets way over by the subway station. At the main entrance, the police had difficulty holding back the flood of students. They let us through the service door. There wasn't a single empty place in the big hall. Gate crashers who made it through sat right on the steps of the amphitheater. What is this, a concert? Yves Montand or an American jazz group on tour? No, it's a poetry reading, our comrades are speaking.

Usually, the organizers of such readings, to avoid unpleasantries later with the City Committee, would throw in among the "unclean" poets a couple of "clean" ones, i.e., those ideologically approved, someone on the lines of Vanshenkin or Firsov. The "clean" ones would open the reading, mumble hurriedly through a poem each and, after sparse applause, get lost real fast. They understood that the audience hadn't come to hear them. And then the main attraction—Andrei

Voznesensky on stage. "Hurrah for the student hot-shots, go on, shoot the Soviet bourgeoisie a good box on the ears... Like the Oshanins[2] kept us from meeting..."

A Soviet poet is reading Soviet verse. Big deal! But the hall catches the subtle allusions and reacts stormily to each sarcastic word. It seems an innocent poem—on soccer. But "... the far left end! Weakest in spirit but really fearsome on the penalty kick..." and the hall goes mad! For the farthest "left" are these favorite poets now on stage. "The right wing moves in to block, he yells hoarsely like a hundred siphons, decorated with a hundred medals, for every leg he's maimed. Left end, my dear, you're playing for your life!" And it isn't necessary to explain anything to the hall, it's so clear who these "right wings" are, decorated with a hundred medals, who maimed so many poets...

In the hall sits Vanya Petrov, or Petya Ivanov, power supply sources student, or university graduate, or young engineer—our coeval, our confederate. One problem disturbs him, as it does us: how are we to live now? When we were growing up, two schizophrenics slaughtered sixty million people. These leaders and führers exchanged experience in the areas of repression and concentration camp management. We were witnesses to the greatest sort of prostitution, called world politics. Everything that was advantageous to our State was declared a righteous and just cause. Everything that was disadvantageous was declared aggression and imperialist intrigues on the part of our neighbors. Never were there so many lies written as in the last twenty years. But even the newspapers could not lie consistently both one way and the other. Five years later they'd say something completely different. This cheap propaganda was designed for fools who wouldn't remember

[79]

even yesterday's paper. But now we all remember, and want to think for ourselves, and don't want others to think for us. They drummed into every one of us: our army is the strongest of all, our ideology is the most advanced, our standard of living is the highest, our government is the wisest. They attempted to make an obedient herd of us—to have us vote, move, approve, guard as one, unanimously, consentiently—in short, we were supposed to be silent pawns on the chessboard of world history, our place was in close ranks, multitudinous and obedient to the will of the ruler. Our job was to march, and they would decide where. But we don't want that, we don't want it!

"Who are we—the pawns or the powerful?" asks Andrei Voznesensky from the stage. "Genius is in the planet's blood. There are no physicists, no lyricists, just Liliputians—or poets."

No, we do not wish to be Liliputians. And those who are determined to beat Liliputian psychology into us, they're... what should we call them exactly...

"O, exact word!—scum! There's such a bustle in their ranks. Their faces dark, and all the same..." reads Bella Akhmadulina. "Everything convenient and edible is drawn to them if not tied down. They're nice to me today, and promise me respect. But their blows are muffled when my time comes..."

They won't let Akhmadulina go—notes, questions, requests to read more. At last they allow her to leave the stage only because Bulat Okudzhava is next.

"But perhaps we're not in a position to do anything?" thinks Vanya Petrov or Petya Ivanov. "Who are we to poke our noses in the higher spheres of politics? We're just simple Soviets after all, they won't let us go anywhere, or do anything."

"If something isn't right—it's not our fault!" sings

Bulat. "As they say, the motherland commands us to... How sweet it is to be guilty of nothing, to be a simple soldier, a soldier..."

As a rule, Evgeny Evtushenko appears at the end. Yes, of course, we follow the rules of the game—sounds the subtext of his poems—they demand of us Bratsk HES, the Komsomol... Naturally, we understand, it can't be any other way just now. Only we're changing everything our own way: "We're dissemblers and iconoclasts, we've tricked the masters, and contrived to follow orders, but do it all backwards. And however much we've risked our necks, or suffered at the hands of enemies or gods, we've acted men and in men seen—gods..."

Among the many poets, good and otherwise, who appeared in the early sixties, five names stood out: Evtushenko, Voznesensky, Rozhdestvensky, Okudzhava, Akhmadulina. From the point of view of their poetic gifts, there were others, probably, and no worse than these, but at that time, no one could compete with the "magnificent pentad." They had the mass audience in their hands, their books were fought over in the stores, it was they who awakened an unprecedented interest in poetry in our country.

But the secret of their success was simple: they were the ones who most boldly expressed aloud the ideas and inspirations of our generation.

Subsequently, Viktor Konetsky declared in an interview with a French journalist, "The older generation grew up in fear, but our generation—in hope and faith." How they berated Konetsky later for these words on various official levels! But then, Konetsky had clearly defined the essence of the early sixties. A short liberal pause, they'd only just exposed the "cult of personality," and already the film "Our Nikita Sergeevich"[3] wasn't far off, but our generation still had hope, it still had hope...

XIV

I am relating events roughly fifteen years past, and much has changed since then. I'm sure that my memoirs will not bring my friends any trouble. Even if they're dragged through the courts, they can always plead that these were the sins of youth, and who didn't sin in their youth.

Before me are books by Robert Rozhdestvensky, which he gave me in those years. (By the way, the inscriptions were torn out at Soviet customs by vigilant officials: now it's forbidden to take not only manuscripts, but inscriptions over the border!) I leaf through the pages... Just as before, I like the northern poems: "There's bad weather over Dickson, a blizzard's hit..." Or the poem about screws: "All the same, they break the desperate ones, all the same you must stay where they screw you in—a primus stove, a watch, a crane, a toilet cover. Disposed so, put in, we won't continue on this theme... Praise the screw psychology! Long reign the slogan: it's not our affair!" But heavens, did I really like all the rest once? Not all, but I liked a lot of it. Rozhdestvensky was strong in his civic poems, he spoke on behalf of his generation; and we were ready then (again I quote Rozhdestvensky) "to take after the Blüchers, the Eichs, the Tukhachevskys..."[1] Alas, our damned ignorance! For us, Eich was a hero of the civil war, a victim of Stalin's terror, and not an obedient executor of Stalin's will, on whose conscience lay the deaths of thousands of dispossessed kulaks.

In all fairness I should note that the name of Rozhdestvensky served as a peculiar sort of shield for writers and poets of the new wave. When they started attacking us in the press for "individualism and lack of ideological content," they usually equivocated, saying they aren't all like that, take Robert Rozhdestvensky.. I remember Robert suffered painfully when the swiftly rising Voznesensky ousted him from second place on the poets' roster. I say second place because Evtushenko was always given first.

It seemed only Chinese guerillas could stop Evtushenko. With amazing ease he got around all official obstacles. There's a plenary session of the Union of Writers coming up. We're all going to get it, but especially Evtushenko. Evtushenko himself flies in the day after from Africa. I tell him about the plenum and add, "The plenum resolved not to print us, and you're at the top of the list." Zhenya is silent and bites his lips dismally. A resolution of the plenum of the Union of Writers... How can we get around it? But a week later a whole column of Evtushenko's poems appears in *Pravda.* All the poems seem part of a series on the friendship of the African peoples with Russia. Who would dare not print it? There's a rumor that Evtushenko has sold out. No, it's just a maneuver. Having "rehabilitated" himself before the official authorities, Evtushenko prints "Babii Yar!" [2] And there's another scandal. And Zhenya's a hero again. And an issue of *The Literary Gazette* with Evtushenko's poems sells for twenty rubles on the black market. That tightrope tactic was successful for a long time. But eventually, they figured him out, and he fell victim to his love of being in the public eye all the time.

[83]

Stop. I guess I've begun to judge from today's perspective. I'd better go back to the notes I made then, on fresh impressions.

So then, Evtushenko, Evgeny Alexandrovich. For some reason, his poetry readings are firmly associated with the mounted police. He is so well-known that, as malicious tongues would have it, if someone steps on his foot on the tram one evening, all the foreign newspapers write about it the next morning. Fantastically hardworking. Only one poem out of seven is good, but since he writes fifty times as much as any of his contemporaries in poetry, he has more good poems than any of them too. However, when he reads them himself, all of his poems seem superb. A marvelous orator, he can carry any audience away with him, even a hostile one. He's hard to take on a personal level, because the basic subject of his conversations is himself. Very unbalanced. Today Evtushenko is sure he is Christ, tomorrow he'll be convinced of his complete insignificance. He gets carried away entirely. In a burst of inspiration he'll be ready to pronounce Anatoly Sofronov a good writer—and sincerely believe it himself for half an hour.

Andrei Voznesensky. The most mysterious person in the Union of Writers. He entered poetry on a parabolic course[3] and still feels that sometimes it "carries him off along the edge somewhere he doesn't want to go." A man of whom there are two diametrically opposed opinions: first, that Voznesensky is a genius; second, that Voznesensky is a dispassionate rogue. Perhaps he likes that childish game of mystery. But precisely because of that, it's difficult to say what will become of him. He could equally well win the Lenin or the Nobel Prize.

Bulat Okudzhava. At school, a boy was asked, "What's your last name?" The boy answered, "I'll tell you, but you'll fall over." His name was Okudzhava. He wasn't related to Bulat at all, but such was Bulat's fame. You can hear tape recordings of Bulat's songs in every city in Russia, in the mines at Chukotka, on the fishing trawlers in Bristol Bay. These songs are not officially recognized as yet; they'll recognize them in about twenty years and put them in anthologies—first of all because they're real songs, and secondly, as usually happens, they'll be used to stifle young minstels of the next generation. (That's what I wrote about the poets twenty years ago. It's interesting that some of it's beginning to come true).

Bella Akhmadulina was accused of trans-sense[4] lyrics and absence of civic feeling. "Oh, haven't I enough other troubles burdening my head; I always dream of little airplanes, and don't know why..." answered Bella. But I recall one instructive episode. There was supposed to be a reception for Steinbeck at the editorial offices of *Youth.* We were all invited, but the editor-in-chief of *Youth,* Boris Polevoi, warned everyone, "Kids, I beg of you, don't put the magazine on the spot, there'll be a representative from the American Embassy with Steinbeck—naturally, a CIA agent—and he'll ask some tricky questions. Don't give in to provocation!" And there in the conference room of *Youth* sits Steinbeck with a shy young American. The embassy employee was silent, while Steinbeck fired questions point-blank, and what questions! They'd have been hard to answer in a one-to-one conversation, but here, in the presence of interested listeners from both intelligence services!... What's more, we're bound by our word. Steinbeck orates, and in answer we mumble something inarticulate. What a stupid situation! But our thanks to Bella, who rescued all of us speechless peasants. She stood up and with her angelic voice explained to Steinbeck in a highly ironic tone the difference between his positions and ours. Apparently, Steinbeck understood everything.

XV

However, before I continue my talk on the writers of my generation, I must recall the situation which had arisen by that time in the Union of Writers and the Moscow Writers' Organization.

The Moscow organization was always off by itself. There were more well-known, talented writers in Moscow than in all the other republics and regions of Russia together. And then the average professional level of the Moscow writers was obviously higher. The party zeal of the literary "generals" ran up against secret or half-open opposition in Moscow. It's no accident then, that in the short thaw of the fifties, Moscow was immediately revivified. Dudintsev's novel *Not By Bread Alone,* published in *New World,* seemed the beginning of a new stage in Soviet literature. The thick anthology *Literary Moscow* disappeared from the book counters in one day. At the plenary session of the Moscow Writers' Organization rang words which the walls of the Central House of Writers hadn't heard in a long while. It got to the point that Prilezhaeva, an old, orthodox Communist, cried out in alarm, "Dudintsev and those who support him are preparing for the American intervention!" Of course, the hall answered her with laughter, but soon after, the incidents in Hungary broke out, and no one felt like making merry.

As everyone knows, writers played a major role

in the Hungarian revolution of 1956. And though the Hungarian poets' polemic with the Soviet tanks ended very fast, "our Nikita Sergeevich" got terribly upset. A burnt child, he dreaded the fire: "Isn't there a branch of Kosszuth's club[1] growing up here, right under our noses in Moscow?" A volley of governmental criticism rained down on the courageous old men of literature. They were forced to beat their breasts at meetings and repent of their mistakes. However, that didn't seem to be enough. One had to contrast "seditious Moscow" with trustworthy, ideologically consistent writers. But where were they supposed to come from? Resolved: we won't set the quality, but the quantity. And then Leonid Sobolev proposed the idea of creating the Union of Writers of the RSFSR.

Leonid Sobolev, who wrote his last book during the war, had been considered retired for a long time. True, he was chairman of the selection committee of the Moscow Writers' Organization, but that pensioner's position couldn't content insatiable ambition, and here was a chance to come out on top. In his ten years of work on the committee, Leonid Sobolev accepted a total of ten persons into the Union of Writers, most on the verge of coronary thrombosis—plus the young Evtushenko. But as we noted earlier, only Chinese guerillas could stop him... However, once at the head of the brand new Union of Writers of the RSFSR, in the course of a year and a half, Sobolev enlisted more than a thousand graphomaniacs into the writers' ranks. The Union accepted prosaists who'd published a thin brochure of sketches in a regional publishing house, poets who had a set of poems printed in a regional newspaper. The basic criterion for the "rite of passage" was place of residence. In Moscow, the selection committee raged on as before, but somewhere off in, say,

Saratov or Rostov-on-the-Don, they took scribblers into the Union of Writers. Naturally, it was politely explained to these new literary geniuses that they'd been expected for ages, but those "Muscovite esthetes" had stood in the way. "Ooooh..." the geniuses ground their teeth, "we'll wrap up Moscow in a jiffy!"

Leonid Sobolev's initiative was immediately supported by the Party. The regional committees competed with each other not so much in meat and milk production as in the number of writers per thousand inhabitants. The principle of industrial production prevailed: The greater the supply, the lower the price. Writers thronged everywhere...

People repeated the statement of the Secretary of the Tula Regional Committee as a joke: "In our region, the cultural life has reached an unprecedented bloom. Before the Revolution, there was one writer in Tula—at Yasnaya Polyanya,[2] and now we have twenty!"

Both the central and the regional press extolled the literati out in the boondocks who lived in close contact with the people and were not subject to Western influence. The regional publishing houses issued in quick succession heavy tomes of the local classics—to the great joy of the salvage collectors. It was just at this time that the all-union paper pulp "golden reserve" was founded.

At the next writers' congress, Moscow elected one delegate for every seven members of the union, and the regional organizations—one out of three. And of course, the congress proceeded in "complete unanimity."

Typically, from then on, it was people from the provinces as a rule who were chosen to "reinforce" the Moscow and central magazines. The critic Yury Barabash, former assistant editor of *The Literary Gazette*, was brought in from Kharkov. They couldn't find an editor-in-chief for *Moscow* magazine in the capital, and summoned Popovkin from Semfiropol; later, Mikhail Alexeev, Sobolev's right-hand man, another non-Muscovite, replaced Popovkin. The current editor of *October,* Ananiev, was invited from Kazakhstan. Dementiev, first assistant to Boris Polevoi at *Youth* is from Kalinin. And even Georgy Markov—current First Secretary of the Union of Writers of the USSR, came straight from Irkutsk.

Under no circumstances do I idealize Moscow writers. Just take Boris Pasternak's expulsion from the Moscow union! True, at the time, volunteers were found to vote for his expulsion "deliberately"; I think that's the only way they could have saved the Moscow organization from complete destruction. But this whole incident with the Union of Writers of the RSFSR clearly showed that the Party was gambling on writers who were less talented, less cultured and more obedient.

The rumble over the Russian writers calmed down all by itself somehow. A few talented names turned up (who would have broken into the central publications in any case); however, the magazines were no longer in any hurry to print the mass of the remaining new-born geniuses. Why? Why, because circulation dropped catastrophically. The reader absolutely refused to buy hack productions. The editors had to employ extraordinary measures—in "subscription months" all the magazines, as if by mutual agreement, released Simenon and Agatha Christie novels. Apparently you can't hold a subscriber without the help of the "decaying West..." And suddenly our literature seemed to get its second wind—the circulation of *Youth* crept up swiftly, there were lines in the libraries for *New World.* Even the orthodox *Banner* revived. The second thaw had come, and along with books by Ilya Ehrenburg, Pavel Nilin and Konstantin Simonov, the first works

[89]

by young Muscovites and Leningraders appeared—
Aksenov, Balter, Bitov, Vladimov, Voinovich, Konetsky, Maximov, Krupnik, Yurian, Semenov...

XVI

I will take the liberty of addressing contemporary
Soviet youth: You've just finished school. You've just
entered college. Perhaps you're just working somewhere on production, but you're all of twenty. You
differ from your contemporaries, who are completely
mad over ice hockey and figure skating, in that you
love to read books. You're not a very experienced
reader and still devour everything as it comes to hand.
And then, quite by accident, you wonder, "What was
our prose like in the early sixties?" An inquisitive
person, you leaf through the recently published *Literary
Encyclopedia.* There, naturally, they speak of the un-
interrupted flowering of Soviet literature. The war
stories of the fifties gave way to the rural prose of the
seventies. But what happened in the sixties? They
refer obscurely to Aksenov's novel *Colleagues;* the
name Yury Kazakov crops up. Maybe that's it. Apparently, there were a couple of lean years there. If
you are meticulous, you'll turn to the monographs of
respected critics. There's a little more information there.
True, you won't once come across the names of Anatoly
Kuznetsov, Maximov, Voinovich, Gladilin (such writers
simply never existed!), but then, for the first time you'll
hear of the so-called "star boys"—heroes of "a series
of prose works of limited ideological content." Where
did these "star boys" come from? Probably, you figure,

from Aksenov's novel *A Ticket to the Stars*. It would be nice to read a little of him! But how? The novella wasn't published as a separate book in our country. And magazines from ten years ago are sent off to the stacks,[1] from which it is very difficult to retrieve them...

For your information, Aksenov's *A Ticket to the Stars* came out in *Youth* magazine in 1961 in an edition of half a million, and was an unprecedented success. They read it in the metro, in the trams, on the street. It was published in thirty countries ("the accursed West" plus Japan). There was even a film made of the book, called *My Younger Brother*. For a whole year *The Literary Gazette* argued over *A Ticket to the Stars* in every issue. Yury Bondarev claimed that he would have taken Aksenov's boys off to the intelligence bureau. "They have no place in Soviet reality!" cried Vasily Smirnov. "Right, boys!" Robert Rozhdestvensky titled his article. "Wrong, boys!" Nikolai Gribachev immediately answered him. Alas, past passions cannot be brought to light now. For all practical purposes, you can't even find the novella.

But then, the appearance of the young prose in the early sixties provoked a bitter debate in the entire Soviet press.[2] I'll give only the extreme opinions. The critic Borshchagovsky, reported to the plenary session of the Moscow Writers' Organization: "Disputing the unity and inseparableness of the ideological and the moral in man, the young literature speaks as the offspring of its time, as a sensitive and well-tuned instrument... The young prose pointedly does not accept a solution to social and spiritual problems in which morality appears in the role of obsequious handmaiden to the so-called business-like man, to worldly, cunning tactics." The critic Boris Pankin of *Komsomol Pravda:*

"A pleiad of young writers has just formed which, using the language of its own heroes, writes 'typical modernities'... The favorite target of many authors and their young heroes is the old philosopher, the old dogmatist, who, tediously and capriciously, tactfully and tactlessly, à propos and non, denounces the young generation, complains it is spoiled, and touchily throws his own and his contemporaries' services in their teeth..."

Borshchagovsky hails a new literary generation: "The young writers struggle against dogmatism in literature more seriously and on a more basic level— by the very fact and nature of their work, by the quests of a hero who thinks, who solves the serious questions of life." Boris Pankin ominously predicts: "It seems the idols are just about to fall from their pedestals."[3]

Such difference in evaluation is not merely a result of the critics' ill will or bias. The books under discussion themselves did not fit in the usual norms of socialist realism. Take, for example, Georgy Vladimov's novella *Pay Lode*. (By the way, the only one of Vladimov's pieces anyone still has anything good to say about.) At first glance, it's a typical production novel in the best Soviet tradition. The main hero, the driver Viktor Pronyakin, makes a decent machine from a wrecked dumptruck and starts to fulfil the plan. However, the dump trucks are still carrying dead rock, and Pronyakin dreams of a pay lode. Finally, the excavator scoop hits a pay lode and Pronyakin, risking his life, attempts to carry it out of the quarry. The risk is too great, and Pronyakin falls, so to speak, at his labor post.

How are critics to resist temptation and not praise the young writer, who glorifies the exploits of the simple Soviet man? But on the other hand, the attentive reader will notice that Vladimov's character is not at all like the typical positive hero. In the first place, he's a good worker, not because he's inspired by the regular appeals from the Party and the government to fulfil the five-year plan ahead of time, but because he simply wants to earn a lot and send for "his old lady" as soon as possible and start living a normal life with her. In the second place, Viktor Pronyakin's good points put him in conflict with the other workers. Everyone around him steals from the department reserves, while Pronyakin carefully saves his dump truck. Pronyakin's desire to make more trips provokes hatred on the part of the entire "fraternal" workers' collective of the "advance brigade." They were used to working in the mine without even rolling up their sleeves, so Pronyakin, you see, stood out. And it turns out that Pronyakin isn't the typical hero of the socialist system, but an exception. For that reason, we perceive Pronyakin's death not as chance, but as law. And of course, once the author has been proven guilty of thus "undermining the very foundations of society," the vigilant critic just tears out his hair.

Much has been written on the young prose of the sixties, and we shall return to these literary debates again. Many opinions were advanced—quite sensitive and quite foolish ones. But personally, it seems to me that the writers of my generation weren't aiming to undermine anything. They simply took up arms with Stendahl's principle: "Literature is a mirror on the highway." They wrote about what they saw. Most likely, they didn't know everything and didn't notice everything. But they wrote honestly and truthfully about what they saw.

At the end of September 1962, the plenary session of the Moscow Writers' Organization convened and seemed to legitimize the appearance of the new generation in literature. Opening the session, the chairman of the governing board of the Moscow Writers' Organization, Stepan Shchipachev said:

> A new generation has arisen, a "youthful, foreign" tribe. They've loudly announced themselves—Anatoly Kuznetsov, Anatoly Gladilin, Evgeny Evtushenko, Georgy Vladimiv, Robert Rozhdestvensky, Yurian Semenov, Georgy Semenov, Eduard Shim, Vladimir Tsybin, Anatoly Poperechny, Vasily Aksenov, Andrei Voznesensky, Svetlana Evseeva, Bella Akhmadulina, Yury Pankratov, Nikolai Antsiferov, Vladimir Firsov, Novella Matveeva and many others. The writers of this generation more and more resolutely win the pages of the thick journals,[4] people write, speak, argue much about them, and sometimes a superfluous hue and cry rises around them...

The official list that Shchipachev read is interesting now because it starts with the names of two writers who have emigrated. But in general, as you may easily imagine, the list was compiled carefully. The names of Maximov, Voinovich and Okudzhava are missing, but Firsov, Pankratov and Poperechny are there, poets who, in my opinion, were no credit to our generation. But it was important for the Moscow Writers' Organization to show that it supported not only "leftists" but "rightists" too. The basic point of Alexander Borshchagovsky's report (on prose) and Yaroslav Smelyakov's (on poetry) comes down to this—that the new generation that had entered literature was our own, a Soviet generation, and there was nothing to fear from them. Borshchagovsky said as much: "The opinion widespread

[95]

among certain critics that our young literature is nihilistic, that it is polemical in regard to the revolutionary past, is seriously in error. It reflects the real literary process, and the inability of certain comrades to understand the process reflects these critics' fear of words, which youth, as we know, does not mince."

One must say finally that the Moscow Writers' Organization actively supported the new generation of writers. I'm convinced that many of the "old men" were sincerely happy with the appearance of young talent. However, the matter got more complex. The administration of the Moscow organization had long been dissatisfied with the domination by the secretariat of the RSFSR. And here an opportunity presented itself to take a peculiar sort of revenge and prove that the promotion of provincial writers was a foolish enterprise which had nothing to do with literature. What's more, with our help, there was the possibility of knocking the orthodox out of the "generalships." So, a hidden polemic with Gribachev, Kochetov, Sofronov and company crept into all the speeches. "These critics," said Borshchagovsky,

> accuse young literature of nihilism, of a certain spiritual unreliability, they suspect it of tendencies toward modernism, toward Westernism, of excessive self-analysis, of a predilection for describing the seamy side of life, of ingratitude in regard to our past, they hint that today's youth is neither one thing nor the other... One would like to ask these writers: do you really read your colleagues' books? And do you recognize in deed, and not merely in word, the right and duty of literature to be diverse, vivid, and self-knowing? The general artistic movement

of the young prose is a denial of dilettantism, of flaccid descriptiveness, of cheerless fiction that has lost even the distraction of plot, a denial of the uncontrolled flood of words, a struggle against the infiltration into prose of common-places, common words, common hackneyed situations. In this sense our young prose is close to the best revolutionary traditions of Soviet literature and polemically is clearly opposed to the flood of mediocre literature which had achieved such wide circulation during the period of the cult of personality.

From the above quotation it is apparent that under the pretext of defending youth, they were attacking the existing order and the whole so-called creative atmosphere that prevailed in our literature.

During the report I for some reason recalled the plenary session of 1957. We, a few students from the institute, broke into the conference hall with difficulty and found seats in the back row. Surkov, Sofronov, Simonov appeared in turn at the podium and thundered against the Moscow writers. (Ah yes, Konstantin Simonov, then editor of *New World,* made a quick 180 degree turn and dumped on Dudintsev.) The writers sat there, heads bowed, cowering, but a few people turned around to us and whispered, "Why don't you object at least! Why don't you whistle! You have nothing to lose!" And we objected, we whistled...

Nothing of the kind happened now. We were given the chance to object and whistle, but from the podium this time. For we still had nothing to lose. And one after another our colleagues went up on stage and spoke in such a manner that Semyon Babaevksy, author of the well-known *Knight of the Golden Star,* who was

[97]

sitting in the presidium, wiped his bald spot again and again, and then simply ran out of the hall.

The plenum concluded triumphantly for us. The old men muttered, smiling, "Be careful, they'll make you secretaries of the Union." Konstantin Simonov, who always had a good sense of direction, clasped Aksenov with one hand, me with the other, and posed for the numerous press photographers. Accounts of the plenum appeared in all the central newspapers.

Something seemed about to happen. The situation was very uncertain—no one knew what would come next, but the ministers started to receive us just in case. I personally was at a reception given by Furtseva and the editor-in-chief of *Pravda,* Satyukov. I remember that Furtseva, who had recently been removed from the Presidium of the Central Committee of the CPSU and appointed Minister of Culture, complained of the injustice of man's fate, and Satyukov promised us all a junket on *Pravda* to any city in the Soviet Union. Personnel changes were in the air. There was talk that it was time for new elections for the secretariat of the Union of Writers of the USSR, and that the most talented and professional writers should manage literature, not respected generals. But the same sort of revolt started up among the cinematographers. In closed session, still underground, they ran Marlen Khutsiev's film *Ilich's Barrier.* Some held that this was a revolution in Soviet cinematography. Passions rose in the Union of Artists too. It all came down to the fact that a sharp change was just about to occur in government policy in the area of literature and the arts. And when the November issue of *New World* appeared with Solzhenitsyn's novella *One Day in the Life of Ivan Denisovich* and Viktor Nekrasov's impressions of America, everyone was already convinced that a liberali-

zation, not only in the area of culture, but in general—
a liberalization of the whole of government policy was
not far off.

I don't wish to portray myself as a prophet, but I
remember perfectly well that even at the September
plenum of the Moscow writers, when the fellows were
going around so proud and independent, and they all
said over and over to each other: "It's an irreversible
process, we've won..."—it seemed to me for some
reason that this was all happening in a sweet dream or
that in a minute the door would open and the ";plain
clothes art critics" would walk in and arrest everybody.

XVII

In the fall of 1961, Ilya Grigorievich Ehrenburg invited Aksenov, Kazakov, Shim and me to his dacha. This meeting of prose writers of the older and younger generations proceeded, as they say in such circumstances, "in a warm and friendly atmosphere," though with the exception of one bit of tactlessness which, naturally, only I could have committed.

"Ilya Grigorievich," I asked without any sort of ulterior motive, "how is it that at the very height of the Stalin terror you were never once arrested?"

Ehrenburg answered very extensively (this answer was included in full in his book *People, Years, Life,* only there he got me mixed up with Aksenov), but the sense of his words came down to this, that in our world you cannot predict nor guess anything in advance.

"In general, everything happens in our country according to a system of chance," continued Ehrenburg, and related the following episode.

After the memorable events of 1956-57, Ehrenburg fell into disfavor too, and his new book *French Notebooks* lay immobilized at the Soviet Writer Publishing House. What's more, as well-wishers passed on, the firm's director, Lesyuchevsky, was definitely against the book's publication. But then there was one of the periodic "high-level" receptions at the Kremlin, to which, among other scientists, artists and writers,

Ehrenburg was invited. After they had delivered the toasts to Mongol-Soviet or Sino-Soviet friendship (I don't remember which), everyone noticed that Khrushchev had stopped Ehrenburg and was chattering away with him about something. The uppercrust-Soviet fête took its course, an atmosphere of warmth and sincerity was evoked by the appropriate beverages, and Khrushchev and Ehrenburg just stood there in the middle of the hall, not moving an inch and talking very animatedly. It continued half an hour, until Mikoyan led Khrushchev away on some diplomatic errand.

The next day, early in the morning, a very upset Lesyuchevsky called Ehrenburg.

"Ilya Grigorievich, we're getting your *French Notebooks* off to the printer on time, but we have a few minor queries...

Ehrenburg, staggered by such a turn of affairs, offered to come to the publishing house himself, but Lesyuchevsky most obligingly proposed sending a courier to Ehrenburg (why should Ilya Grigorievch trouble himself?). In short, the *French Notebooks* were published in two months.

"What did you talk to Khrushchev about?" one of us asked.

"A subject that had nothing to do with literature," Ehrenburg answered. "We just told each other how each of us physically perceived the approach of old age, but this innocent conversation had an unexpected result. Apparently, someone reported back to Lesyuchevsky and he decided to cover himself just in case."

I recalled this story of Ehrenburg's for this reason: it might appear that in my accounts I over-exaggerate the role of the period's young writers in the stormy events of the early sixties. The reasonable question arises—were we really braver or wiser or craftier than the writers of the older generation? Of course not, naturally the oldsters were wiser and understood what was going on better than we; however, all their life's experience suggested that it is stupid to hope for a logical order of things in our country, and if something happens, it's just according to a system of chance. But we, the young writers, lacked this experience, and it seemed to us that everything develops naturally and could be no other way. The oldsters remembered how they had been "beaten" and knew that when you're beaten, it's rather painful. Practically speaking, we hadn't really been beaten yet, and so we barged straight ahead. It wasn't just Khrushchev's reforms, but the literary revolt of the youth that provoked the appearance in print of Solzhenitsyn's *One Day in the Life of Ivan Denisovich.* However, after *Ivan Denisovich,* the atmosphere changed abruptly. We were calling for a revolution in literature, but Solzhenitsyn in fact called for a revolutionary transformation of society. True, there were no direct revolutionary appeals in Solzhenitsyn's novella, but *Ivan Denisovich* transferred the emphasis of the struggle from literature to politics. And, of course, the foundations really started shaking then.

The mighty Party machinery started to worry. Reciprocal measures would have to be taken immediately. What measures? Solzhenitsyn enjoyed "high-level patronage" and for the moment was untouchable. But it was essential to indicate that the Party machinery had adroitly kept its bearings. Apparently, that's when the idea of compromising the creative youth was born. In two days "art lovers" from the Central Committee organized an exhibition of artists in the Manège.[1]

On December 1, 1962, "our Nikita Sergeevich" appeared at the exhibition in the Manège, already in the appropriate mood. "Where are these abstractionist daubers and pederasts?" he started yelling from the doorway. "The collective Party leadership" moved in close ranks behind Khrushchev and smirked gloomily. The young artists, many of whom were exhibiting their work for the first time, were simply crushed by the force of this comradely criticism.

"Must we drive you from our Soviet land!" Khrushchev shrieked. "We'll go buy you all tickets over the border."

"Up to the border," State Security Committee (KGB) Chairman Semichastny corrected precisely.

Only one man dared to argue with the Central Committee General Secretary and Chairman of the Soviet of Ministers of the USSR, but he argued desperately, viciously. He was the sculptor Ernst Neizvestny.

Years passed, and the modest retiree Khrushchev, dismissed from all his posts, called Ernst and apologized for the Manège incident. Years passed, and the family of the deceased Khrushchev asked Neizvestny to create a monument for Nikita Sergeevich's grave. And crowds of pilgrims came to Novodevichi Cemetery[2] to look at that monument—the bald head on two pieces of marble, black and white.[3]

Characteristically, in the Russian folk epos, the national hero is Ivan the fool. His older brothers, sly and evil, usually make fools of themselves, and Ivan the fool always wraps them around his little finger and almost playfully conquers evil. Khrushchev did our country much good, possibly without realizing it himself. Like a true hero of the *bylinas*,[4] he adroitly dealt with the mighty Beria, brought down the "anti-Party faction" and took on Stalin's direct heirs. But, obviously, in our time it's hard for a man with a fourth-

[103]

grade education to govern the country, even if he is well-grounded in Marxism. It's difficult now to imagine where the Khrushchev reforms would have led, if that ill-starred exhibition in the Manège hadn't turned up. But they'd calculated well! A man for whom the height of art was the song "Rushnichok" naturally had to go into a frenzy over the trans-sense paintings of left-wing artists. How can one help but mention here the Russian story-teller's embellishment, "they tricked the fool on every hand..."

Someone has always threatened the Soviet state: the Entente, Kolchak, Denikin,[5] the Trotskyites, the Zinovievites, the left opposition, the right deviationists, the kulaks, the kulaks' henchmen, the enemies of the people, idolators of the West or of everything foreign, the modernist composers, the Mendel-Morganists, the killer-doctors, and then simply the beatniks. Usually, when they investigated the next failure in industry or agriculture, they immediately found the culprits among the intelligentsia. And so, at the end of 1962, the entire Party and Soviet press harmoniously trumpeted forth the new danger—vile abstractionists.

XVIII

The wave raised by the liberalization could not be quelled at a single blow. Three months passed after the scandal at the Manège, during which time no one could say with any certainty where it would all lead.

On December 17, 1962 in the Palace of Receptions, the so-called conference of Party and government with the creative intelligentsia took place. As Solzhenitsyn recalls, first of all the creative intelligentsia was fed a seven-course dinner. Khrushchev was in a very equable mood. True, he swore as much as before when mentioning the abstract artists, but without his earlier malice. And then, Khrushchev apologized to Margarita Aliger for shouting at her in 1957. Later, Nikita Sergeevich gave valuable comments regarding Marlen Khutsiev's film *Ilich's Barrier.*

"It was great when one of those scum got it in the teeth," Khrushchev declared, "only they should have beat him harder."

This profound idea became the basis of a series of reviews that soon appeared in the press. The film was panned nation-wide, though it hadn't yet gone out to the country's movie screens. Movie-goers only saw Khutsiev's work two years later. The film was cut, distorted, central scenes replaced. Director friends simply stole Khutsiev's picture and managed to insert cinematic finds from *Ilich's Barrier* into their own films. Khutsiev's film came out under a different title, *I'm Twenty*. The perplexed viewer would shrug his shoulders, unable to understand what exactly had set the whole forest ablaze. And then, by the time the film hit the screen, it had really gone out of date. The sharp questions Khutsiev asked two years before now seemed naive—after all, an answer had been given, and a very unequivocal one.

On December 1, 1962, Khrushchev put the "left-wing artists" to complete rout. On December 17, trampling Khutsiev's motion picture, Khrushchev broke the spine of Soviet cinematography. However, the liberals among the writers and artists left the Palace of Receptions in an optimistic mood: and well they might, for Nikita Sergeevich had demonstratively shaken Solzhenitsyn's hand and had stood with him before numerous movie- and photo-lenses. So, all is not yet lost! At the end of December, CPSU Ideological Secretary Ilichev organized a two-day conference with young writers at the Central Committee. They hadn't touched the young literature yet; they were sounding it out. Our lads put up a good show, and Robert Rozhdestvensky's speech was simply beautiful. But then, the most amazing thing occurred. The poet Vladimir Firsov unexpectedly attacked Stepan Shchipachev, the First Secretary of the Moscow branch of the Union of Writers, accusing him of an attempt to "disarm youth ideologically." A curious detail: a few months before this, Firsov was to have been taken into the army for active service, his deferment had run out. Firsov ran "weeping and sobbing" to Shchipachev. Shchipachev came to the young poet's rescue, that is, he in fact helped Firsov to desert from the army. Now Firsov showed his gratitude to his benefactor. Firsov's action seemed so absurd to everyone that even Ilichev winced.

"Everyone gives bad speeches, it's not worth paying attention to them," said the Central Committee Secretary, but he took Firsov's name. In March 1963, when the next pogrom started in the Moscow Writers' Organization, Firsov moved up fast.

This incident shows that there were some sharp fellows among the young writers—they knew how to make a career.

As Solzhenitsyn recalls, "The second Kremlin assembly of March 7-8, 1963 was one of the most shameful pages in the whole Khrushchev administration. The Stalinists created a fivefold majority (they invited *apparatchiks*[1] and regional committee members) and the atmosphere was one of savage howling and the devastation of everything that smacked at all of freedom."

The first day of the conference, March 7, presaged no storms. True, the creative intelligentsia was not given dinner. The second day, March 8, proceeded according to a well-developed scenario. Wanda Vasilevskaya got up to the podium. We imagined she would wish the company many happy returns of International Women's Day. But no, the aged writer, on the verge of tears, informed the hall that she'd just returned from Poland, and the Polish comrades had complained to her that certain young Moscow writers were preventing fraternal Poland from building Socialism.

"Their names!!!" howled the hall in concert.

"Why so fast?" said Vasilevskaya coyly from the podium.

"Give their names!" bellowed Nikita Sergeevich.

"Very well," answered Vasilevskaya obligingly. "Voznesensky and Aksenov."

"Voznesensky to the podium!" howled the two thousand in the hall, the flower of Soviet intelligentsia and ideology.

Pale, Voznesensky rose to the podium and began with the words, "Like my great teacher Mayakovsky, I'm not a Party member..."

"So you're proud of it?" Khrushchev broke in. The hall was raving like the Roman Coliseum in anticipation of the gladiators' blood. Voznesensky was interrupted incessantly. Finally Voznesensky asked to be allowed to read some poetry. The flower of the intelligentsia objected loudly, but Khrushchev graciously permitted it. Voznesensky read the poem "Lenin's Sequoia."

"Well, okay," said Nikita Sergeevich, "the poem's not bad, but anyway—you work with us and we'll back you up. Turn against us—and we'll chop you to pieces! Here's my hand!"

The hall, a bit annoyed that no bloodshed had occurred, demanded Aksenov.

"There he is!" yelled Khrushchev, pointing at a young bearded man in a red sweater. "I noticed him a long time ago—everyone applauds but him!"

The man Khrushchev pointed at was literally dragged from his seat to the podium. It was the artist Illarion Golitsyn.

"You're taking revenge on us for your father!" yelled Khrushchev, without even letting Golitsyn open his mouth.

"What father?" asked Golitsyn. "My father's alive, and anyway, I'm not Aksenov."

Ilichev slipped from his place and whispered something in Khrushchev's ear.

"Okay, sit down," growled Khrushchev to Golitsyn, "here's my hand!"

And Ilichev announced in an icy voice, "Comrade Aksenov has the floor."

As Aksenov told it later, he thought the floor was falling away beneath his feet as he walked to the podium. He doesn't remember how he started his speech. Khrushchev, red as a beet, pounded his fist, spewed saliva, and interrupted Aksenov at every phrase. Aksenov expected in a moment the order would be given, and the hall would tear him to pieces. Khrushchev's words reached him as if out of a fog.

"You're taking revenge on us for your father's being executed!"

"Nikita Sergeevich," said Aksenov, "my father is an old Communist, he was rehabilitated, he's alive, and we associate his rehabilitation with your name."

And once again Ilichev slipped from his place and whispered something to Khrushchev.

"Okay," Nikita Sergeevich changed his tone, "if you're with us, we'll help you, turn against us and we'll annihilate you! But for now, go, and work—here's my hand!"

The solemn conference drew to a close. In the corridor, Aksenov, Voznesensky and film director Arseny Tarkovsky stood apart, completely shaken. The close ranks of the flower of the creative intelligentsia and the Party machine poured past them. They looked askance at the three renegades, as if they had the plague, and hurried into the other hall where richly laden banquet tables stood in all their beauty. Only Nikolai Gribachev paused by Voznesensky and condescendingly clapped him on the shoulder.

"What can you do, old boy? Life changes faster than we expect."

And Gribachev followed into the hall—to wash down the victory. The liberalization in Russia was through. As they said long ago in Odessa, "the old girl didn't suffer long at the villain's experienced hands."

[109]

I never took part in a single high- or mid-level assembly myself. Why not? The answer seems simple enough—I was never invited. But if you investigate this question thoroughly, I probably did everything possible to keep myself on the sidelines. In this case, it's apparent from my example how conformist thinking develops.

Imagine the following picture: Anatoly Sofronov offers his play to the Vakhtangov Theater.[2] Usually authors bring their plays to the *zavlit*[3] and agonize for several months in uncertainty. But the outstanding Soviet playwright Sofronov acts differently. He invites the theater management to his apartment and reads the play himself. And here's Sofronov's apartment, Anatoly Vladimirovich is declaiming his usual concoction, and the theater managers (all national artists of the USSR or honored artists of the Republic) are languishing from boredom and watching their chief director Ruben Nikolaevich Simonov. National Artist of the USSR Ruben Simonov turns one eye on Sofronov, the other to the dining room, where on a white table cloth, in sumptuous serving pieces, there's *balyk*,[4] caviar, salmon and a battery of bottles. That's Sofronov's tradition—after the reading, the inevitable banquet. For about an hour Ruben Simonov is tormented by his ambivalence, he swallows and suddenly explodes, "Enough, I'm sick of listening to that mess! We're not going to stage your play, we're going to stage Gladilin's."

Simonov stands up, and leaves without shaking Sofronov's hand. And after him—the whole theater management. Naturally, the young Vakhtangovites, admirers of my play, informed me of this incident in detail. Two days later I was invited to the theater, to a general meeting of the troupe. A triumphal reading of my play. Yulia Borisova, then still an honored artist of the republic, just said right out, "To the great playwrights of all times—Shakespeare, Molière and Gladilin." I swear, I'm not joking! And then, it was pronounced with a good deal of passion, with tears in the voice. In the theater—jockeying for position, intrigues over the assignment of parts. But Ruben Nikolaevich warned me confidentially, "Tolya, your play will be a new phase for us. But one favor—don't put us in a spot. Keep it quiet."

Just then, a Polish journalist arrives who has interviews with Voznesensky and Aksenov—the very interviews so successfully employed by Wanda Vasilevskaya at the conference of government and intelligentsia on March 8. The Polish journalist tells me through Aksenov that he wants to meet me. But I refuse, for I'd promised to keep it quiet.

Youth magazine is preparing my novella *First Day of the New Year* for publication; the novella broke through the editorial barrier with great difficulty. Editor-in-chief Boris Polevoi's first reaction to my things was usually thus: "Over my dead body!" But later, after long emendations of the manuscript, Polevoi would be convinced. What's more, the novella sharply criticized procedures in the Union of Artists, and Polevoi had his own personal score with the Academy of Arts. The scandal in the Manège wasn't in the air yet, and Polevoi apparently decided to slap the Academy with my hand. After December 1, 1962, that is after Manège, my novella was tied up once again; but for Polevoi, who had declared himself the most daring person on the editorial board, it was now too embarrassing to back down. *Youth's* editorial board talked me into going off to Yalta, to the house of creativity,[5] away from events in Moscow.

So I'm sitting in Yalta writing a new novel. At the end of December I receive a telegram from the governing board of the Union of Writers: "Return to Moscow immediately for conference with Central Committee. Fare and expenses at public cost." I phone *Youth.* They beg me not to come.

"Tolya, we know your indiscreet tongue, you'll spoil everything for us."

"But why?" I ask. "Aksenov can be there but not me?"

"Because Aksenov's *Oranges from Morocco* is already signed through for publication, but your manuscript hasn't passed the censor yet."

Highly disciplined, I sit in Yalta writing a novel. But at the beginning of January my nerves give out, I fly to Moscow. I go to *Youth's* editorial offices straight from the airport. In Polevoi's office I see the following scene: the boss is toiling by the sweat of his brow, rewriting my novella for me right on the galleys. I manage to save some things—others not. And once again they're talking me into something:

"Tolya, we're doing the best we can! The most important thing is for the novella not to be cut from the February issue."

A great temptation! *Youth* hadn't printed me for two years. It was sort of stupid to miss an opportunity to hit the half-million mark in circulation.

The first issue of *Youth* for 1963 comes out with Aksenov's novella *Oranges from Morocco.*[6] The press attacks it headlong. True, they didn't trample it underfoot yet, the "trampling" order would be given after March 8.

Not long ago, I was rereading *Oranges from Morocco.* A well-written, romantic, absolutely pro-Soviet piece. One wonders why they smeared it so. I've come to the conclusion that if there ever really were enemies of the poeple in our country, they usually sat (and sit) in the ideological and cultural departments of the Central Committee and in the administration of the creative unions, newspapers, and magazines. I swear, only on a job for "enemy intelligence" could you make the honest works of Soviet writers out to be the bogy of ideological sabotage. It seems that high-placed government bureaucrats consider it their basic task to embitter the writers. By the way, I am ready to argue that Pasternak's celebrated *Doctor Zhivago* is a novel more acceptable to the Soviet regime than even *The Quiet Don.* And if there'd only been a man upstairs who'd been the least interested in Soviet literature, there wouldn't have been the embarrassment over the Nobel prize or the personal tragedy of Pasternak himself.

Okay, it's a thing of the past... In February 1963, *Youth* came out with my novella, and bumps and bruises came down on me too. The magazine, following its tradition of avoiding open confrontations, again sent Aksenov and me away from Moscow. We sat in Riga reading about how they were working us over in the press, and every day there were delegations from institutes, from universities to see us, and every day we spoke in auditoriums packed with young people, and every day we were convinced that our books were needed, that they did something useful. If there ever was a happy time in my life, it was probably those two weeks.

But the *i's* hadn't been dotted yet, and suddenly I was appointed a member of the editorial college and editor of the Gorky film studio.

I wasn't invited to the conference of Party, government and intelligentsia on March 7-8. Perhaps I just didn't rank, or perhaps they recalled my refusal to take part in the conference at the Central Committee. On March 8, I was sitting with my friends in the House of Writers impatiently waiting for the results of the high-level conference. The CHW had the day off, celebrating International Women's Day. And the fellows still weren't back... At last Aksenov appeared. He looked awful. He wouldn't answer my questions. I dragged him up to the bar by force, poured him a tall glass of cognac and made him drink. Only then did his eyes take on a conscious expression and he muttered, "It's all over, a complete defeat."

XIX

In the course of a few months, beginning December 1, 1962, Khrushchev literally trampled underfoot everything new that had appeared in Soviet painting, cinema and literature. It seems to me that the all-powerful Secretary of the Central Committee of the CPSU and Chairman of the Soviet of Ministers was himself just a toy in the capable hands of the conservative Party machine and admirers of Stalin. Khrushchev supposed that he was waging war with the abstractionists and modernists, but in essence he was halting the de-Stalinization process which he himself had started. Naturally, the exultation of the Stalinists knew no bounds. Here is the orthodox writer Vasily Smirnov's commentary on the events of March 8, 1963 from the pages of the *Literary News:*

> In the lives of each of us there are events which leave an indelible trace, which are engraved in our memory forever, which strengthen us and our spiritual forces in the dearest, innermost parts of ourselves, for the sake of which we exist on this earth, work and live. Just such an event, forever a part of our spiritual life, was the last conference of the creative intelligentsia with Party and government leaders, a great decisive colloquy on fundamental questions

of the development of Soviet arts and letters, and most important—the unforgettable moment of this conference—the lucid, profound, stirring speech of Nikita Sergeevich Khrushchev.

What a style! After shedding a few tears over that "lucid, profound, stirring speech," Vasily Smirnov proceeds to the point of the discussion.

"Unfortunately, the education of our young authors in this country does not always prove to be what the people and Party require." And then, fearing nothing any longer, Vasily Smirnov, in the name of the Party and the people, starts dashingly to wield his critical truncheon. I catch it in this article too, so I won't continue the quotation; but this article is typical. In a short space of time, dozens of these articles appeared, and then hundreds. Voznesensky and Aksenov were declared the chief sinners, and soon Evtushenko's name was added to theirs. It wasn't the right time for him to have published his *Autobiography* in the West.

At the Union of Writers several plenary sessions in a row passed. The orthodox spoke indignantly from the podium: why, they asked, are Evtushenko and Voznesensky allowed to go abroad? By the way, it was just then that our poetry gained great popularity overseas—our young poets read to packed halls. But who would come to hear Vasily Smirnov or, say, Lev Oshanin? But the question of the "usefulness" of such trips occupied no one; it was important to denounce the "internal enemies" as loudly as possible. After the Pasternak affair, I don't recall a noisier crew.

A palace revolution was carried out even in the Moscow Writers' Organization. The old secretary was driven out for "corrupt liberalism"; and even the

Moscow Writers' Party organization, since it hadn't justified the great confidence entrusted it, was disbanded. Now the Moscow writers had to register with the Party at the HUOs,[1] at the construction offices, at the shoe-repair shops and even at the Zoo. This all came under the slogan "Writers—closer to life!"

Now put yourself in the place of the scapegoats, that is, the now disgraced writers and artists. You get the feeling one fine day that your telephone has been disconnected. Earlier, the telephone strained itself—calls from publishers, theaters... Then all at once it stopped short. Publishers and magazines hastily return your manuscripts, and the theaters—the theaters, of course, have started rehearsing plays by Sofronov and Solodar again. That's when the stratification began in our generation. True, the majority of the fellows maintained a blank silence, but some were found who quickly published their jingoistic works. It was fine to be considered left-wing when it brought popularity, but leftishness became dangerous; and so the writers, and especially the critics who had recently glorified the younger generation in the press, quickly began to retract and repent their mistakes.

But what is significant is this: in Khrushchev's time the disgraced intelligentsia were beaten, but not given the final blow. For example, Vasily Grossman's novel *In a Just Cause* was put out of circulation by our "unsleeping agents," but the author himself was not arrested. The sculptor Ernst Neizvestny was torn to pieces almost every day in the newspaper, but they didn't kick him out of the studio, and didn't expel him from MOSA.[2] And as soon as the sensation in the papers had abated, new poems by Voznesensky, Evtushenko, Okudzhava, Akhmadulina began timidly to appear. Even the long-suffering film *I'm Twenty*

[117]

came out (the mutilated version of Marlen Khutsiev's *Ilich's Barrier*). Apparently, Nikita Sergeevich retained a natural, peasant attitude toward his household. Oh yes, the whole country was his patrimony, and we were included. A peasant might tear out the whole vegatable garden, stupidly confusing healthy herbs with weeds, but he'll be careful not to smooth it over with asphalt.

We sensed the change in state policy and many of us wrote letters to Ilichev, then ideological secretary. And curiously enough, some of us who had just recently been nationally disgraced were promised that our stories would be published. And I would note further that in Khrushchev's time these promises were kept, despite opposition from the Stalinist machine. So, for example, the director of the Soviet Writer Publishing House Lesyuchevsky, a man who "sent up" many writers in 1937, candidly declared to Aksenov in a private conversation that he was categorically against Aksenov's *Oranges from Morocco,* but as a Communist he was compelled to obey the order of the Central Committee Secretary.

Our Nikita Sergeevich just couldn't possibly manage to surpass America in meat and milk production; what's more, he wasn't able to cope with the chronic difficulties in agriculture. While Khrushchev was planting corn and complicating matters with the virgin soil,[3] while he was removing the mummified Stalin from the mausoleum, while he was searching for culprits among the "anti-Party group and those attached to it," while he was denouncing abstract artists and modernist writers, the Party machine was chuckling indulgently. For in principle, all of Khrushchev's reforms reinforced the power of the Party machine in the provinces. But then, completely desperate, Nikita Sergeevich began to shake the Party machine itself. They could not forgive him that.

The details of the anti-Khrushchev conspiracy are well known. It's interesting that the Moscow intelligentsia greeted this coup d'état in rather humdrum fashion, and without even any particular enthusiasm. It would seem they would have been glad. After all, Khrushchev had managed to spite everyone. And yet no wild rejoicing was observed. All our liberals, as if by agreement, repeated the same phrase. "The next one won't be any better!"

XX

In 1964 I wrote the novel *The Story of a Circle.*
With it, I bid farewell to the youth theme. It was a
summing up of the youth of my generation. The majority of my contemporaries were more or less well
set up, received pretty good salaries, and youthful
rebellious ideas had given place to domestic problems
and concern over careers. Just a few, honest and restless fellows, were as keenly agitated as before over the
issues of the day. They avoided compromise, and so
could not find themselves a suitable place in Soviet
reality. That, actually, is what the novel was about.
It seemed entirely "passable" to me, for in the circle
I told about, the fate of all the characters except one
was happy. True, that one—Ruslan Zvonkov—was
the central character in the novel.

Naturally, *Youth's* editor-in-chief, Boris Polevoi,
greeted *The Story of a Circle* with the words, by this
time traditional, "Over my dead body!" But the novel
found an active defense on the editorial staff. What's
more, it was a vague, transitional period (Khrushchev
had just fallen, and the new collective leadership as yet
refrained from fundamental directives on literary
themes), and for that reason, Polevoi could be pressed
by public opinion. They promised Polevoi that Gladilin's novel could be "ironed out"[1] so that there'd
be no trouble for the magazine.

In the half-century of its existence, the Soviet regime has worked with writers in different ways. Writers have been shot, sent to concentration camps, stifled with hunger and silence, their manuscripts have been seized, their books mutilated by the censor's scissors, or simply not printed. Something of this diverse arsenal fell even to my lot. The editor's galoshes ran even through my manuscripts. But in our liberal times a new method of taming obstinate writers had been worked out. In the example of *The Story of a Circle* the essence of this method is clear.

I had attached to me a personal editor, a very nice, intelligent man, who understood everything, smilingly fished out all the hints and subtexts, showered compliments and would say, for example, the following:

> Anatoly Tikhonovich, I'm not arguing with you over the essence, but let's run through it phrase by phrase. Why tease the geese? What's the point of this analogy? After all, both you and I are interested in having the novel see the light of day. Take out this word here, take out this expression here... You see, everything's quieter, it doesn't annoy anybody! Why are you so attached to that passage? That's no turning point in world literature, and Polevoi's sure to have a fit. Scratch that paragraph, okay? Lovely!

And that every day for two months, debates over every page. At first I argue, and then I get dazed and don't understand anything. The editor is in a sweat, he's in ecstasy, he's toiling, he sincerely wishes me well. It seems to be stylistic correction... But literature is the word, words are removed and the sense of the novel changes.

The Story of a Circle was printed in *Youth* magazine in fall 1965, a print-run of half a million. The novel, much combed and brushed, at first solicited favorable comment in the press. Just then, Soviet Writer Publishing House put out my novella *First Day of the New Year* in book form. As I've already told you, this piece had been published in *Youth* as well, in Khrushchev's time, and underwent sharp criticism. But it was published now, probably, precisely for that reason. And once again the Vakhtangov Theater rehearsed my long-suffering play.

Controlled by invisible strings, Fortune once again clearly turned her face to me; and who knows, perhaps they were even ready to canonize me as a "Soviet classic." In any case, they showed me the galleys of a long and good article in *Komsomol Pravda* devoted to *The Story of a Circle.*

However, that article never quite saw the light of day. There was a plenary session of the Komsomol Central Committee at which First Secretary of the All-Union Leninist Communist Youth League Sergei Pavlov unexpectedly came down on *The Story of a Circle,* declaring that American imperialist intrigues and Gladilin's works were impeding the Communist education of youth. Why did he say that? To what end? My novel, I repeat, came out in a quite pale version. Pavlov's attacks seemed unfair even to so cautious a man as Konstantin Simonov. Simonov even wrote an article in the *Komsomol* in which, with reservations, he defended my novel. Sergei Pavlov in turn wrote an answer. This polemic should have appeared in the paper, but again, it did not. Probably, somewhere upstairs, they decided that the discussion would only attract attention to *The Story of a Circle.* After

Khrushchev's slating, our higher-ups had learned something. Experience in the ideological struggle suggested
that unnecessary stir increased a writer's popularity.
So they acted more simply with me and stopped printing altogether. *The Story of a Circle* turned out to be
my last book on the contemporary scene published
in the Soviet Union.

It has been held that the Komsomol Central
Committee has considered it its legitimate right to
manage the literary life of the country. This management has been very specific and is described in Osip
Mandelstam's *The Fourth Prose*.[2]

> Vasenka's just about to hit into him, and
> the old maids, vile hags, nudge each other and
> hold the lousy coachman's son down.
> "Hit him, Vasenka, hit him, and we'll hold
> golden boy down, we'll caper all around..."
> What is this? A genre-painting of the Venetsia-
> nov school?[3] A study by some serf artist?
> No, it's the training of a shockheaded Kom-
> somol kid under the guidance of his agitprop[4]
> mamas, grannies and nursies, so that he, Vasen-
> ka, will stomp him, so that he, Vasenka, will
> hit into the bugger while we hold him down,
> while we caper all around...
> "Hit him, Vasenka, hit him..."

The Komsomol's role as young Master Vasenka,
who can hit into people with impunity, became traditional in Soviet "ideological performances." How often
the instigators of the regular teeth-smashing campaigns
were the so-called Komsomol volunteers! By the way,
the first to demand the poet Boris Pasternak's expulsion
from the Soviet land if he accepted the Nobel Prize was

Secretary of the Komsomol Central Committee Semichastny.

Of course, Sergei Pavlov, like any other high-placed Soviet bureaucrat, never wrote his own speeches. Speeches are usually written by assistants, and the bureaucrat himself only gives instructions, corrects and declaims these speeches from the podium. But I doubt that in my case it was the initiative of a reviewer. Pavlov had never missed an opportunity to light into my books before. Apparently he had something against me.

In any case, contemporary writer Gladilin was shut down, completely this time.

The future careers of Komsomol Central Committee first secretaries usually developed as follows: department head in the Party Central Committee, and then—Secretary of the Central Committee of the CPSU (as with Mikhailov) or Chairman of the KGB (as with Shelepin and Semichastny). But Sergei Pavlov had extraordinarily bad luck. He didn't land in the Central Committee or the KGB, and he tried so hard! Why? Perhaps they were getting even with the "rosy-cheeked Komsomol leader" for his incompetence in literary matters? No, it's all much simpler. The auditing commission disclosed that Pavlov himself and his closest Komsomol associates took part of their salary in certificates, i.e., they stole state *valyuta!*[5]

Speculation in *valyuta* is looked upon severely in our country; valyuteers go to prison. Pavlov's career was cut short and he was sent off... to be Chairman of the Gymnastics and Sports Committee of the Soviet of Ministers of the USSR.

XXI

Writers of my generation are closely tied to the theater world. We were breaking our own road through to literature; and our contemporaries, the famous actors and directors of the future, battled with the theatrical stereotypes, tried to stage good plays and sometimes even managed to found their own theater as, for example, with The Contemporary. For reasons easily surmised, I cannot give my actor friends' names. Alas, any indiscreet word from me could impede their current work. But I should say something in general about the theatrical world in which they live.

So, the typical big-city theater. Stanislavsky said that theater begins with the cloak room. However, that is for the audience. For a person connected with the art world, theater begins with the chief director. The chief is always a very respected and very famous actor and director of the past. The chief always leads new undertakings in the life of the theater. The chief always, at all times, loves and supports youth (even when there's a sixty-year-old celebrity playing Juliet). The chief always makes comments to the point, always finds unexpected solutions, and after each of the chief's remarks, the actors loudly sigh, "That's great! Why didn't we see that before!" True, behind the scenes, in the small dressing rooms, having cautiously checked the hall and locked the door tight, the young actors often mimic the chief and imitate his favorite gestures and intonations. But that is probably a result of inexperience or of great love for the boss.

The second man in the theater is the director. His sphere is the paperwork for the actors' trips abroad. The director loves to make himself out to be a man of great erudition and a subtle connoisseur of the theater, but only until the chief looks into his office. In the chief's presence, the director, as a rule, keeps quiet, looks out the window distractedly or drums on the table with his fingers, repeating, "Yes, yes, very true..." At the most critical discussions on a new play, or during disputes over an actor's work, an expression of a peculiar indifference and even boredom never leaves the director's face. But the director immediately comes to life when it's a question of personal matters. Then he becomes feverishly active.

There are superstars and simply stars. The superstars are the National Artists of the USSR or the RSFSR. They have private theater dressing rooms, each of which has an in-house telephone. Often, for one reason or another (usually nervous upset resulting from intensive intrigue), the superstars cannot appear in a performance. The whole theater learns of it instantly, and the director calls the superstars at home, cries and sobs into the receiver, begs them to somehow summon all their strength and take part in the performance—otherwise, the whole of Soviet art will perish that very evening. After those words, the superstars graciously consent, and the director, with a practiced movement, wipes his forehead with a handkerchief.

The simply-stars are, as a rule, Honored Artists of the Tadzhik, Mordvinian or Kabardino-Balkarsk Republics. Photos of the simply-stars are in a prominent place in the foyer of the theater. But they don't neglect their roles, for the director will quickly find a young replacement for them, and that always means...

Beyond that, actors are divided into categories by the pay scale, though the very lowest by wage rate come to the theater early in the morning and return home late in the evening, because they appear in all the performances—either in episodic roles, or as silent soldiers or students, or they simply organize stunt shows backstage. Their position is very complicated: they're busier than anyone else, and they're paid all of eighty rubles a month.[1] And so, during the day, on the central squares of regional hamlets, at markets, at hairdresser's shops, on trains, in housing offices, consumer service complexes,[2] wherever the radios are never turned off,[3] these actors speak in the voices of foxes, bunnies, gray wolves, hunters, oppressed Negroes, American plantation owners, Red partisans, Pioneers, old landed gentry, Cuban peasants and free patriots in radio shows. But even these actors, the lowest on the pay scale, arouse unconcealed envy in a great number of young and old failures from the provinces, who dream of landing in a big-city theater even as an extra.

When a playwright brings his play to the theater, he usually associates with the head of the literary department *(zavlit)*. The *zavlit* never says he likes a play until both the director and a few members of the artistic committee like it. The *zavlit* says the play is good when the chief likes it. However, it's still too early for the author to rejoice. The play must pass the Cultural Administration of the Moscow Municipal Executive Committee and the Central Directorate[4] — only then does the *zavlit* congratulate the author and say that he has written a very important piece. But that's not all. The play must receive the official stamp of the Ministry of Culture of the RSFSR and the USSR, only then does the *zavlit* warble and assure the playwright that the play is marvelous. And still it's too early for the author to celebrate—the play does not yet have "LIT," that is, it hasn't passed the censor.

At last the play is approved, the actors have learned their parts, all the sets are prepared, the director has found his two "only artistic solutions," the chief has made his brilliant comments, the dress rehearsal approaches—can you congratulate the author? No! For at the last run-through, like a bolt from the blue, the Executive Commission from the Party Moscow Regional Committee descends—and the show is closed for good.

You don't envy the playwright. And the actors and directors? It's even worse for them. The playwright can hide the play in his desk, in the hope that grateful future generations in the next millenium will find this manuscript and appreciate it. But where is an actor to hide his talent? Who can see the part he never played? Who can appreciate the director's talent if he's not allowed to stage the show? It's a good thing that there are Russian and foreign classics, that is, plays that, say, two hundred years ago received the approval of LIT and the ministry. But the cultural administration demands that contemporary life be shown on stage. And the directors stage plays by Sofronov and Solodar, and the actors struggle with roles of *Chekists*[5] and collective-farm workers. What else is there to do? A person has to live. The theater, like literature is always forced to compromise—let's do Mikhalkov, and then, who knows, they might suddenly pass a play by some young, "left-wing" playwright of ours, or a contemporary foreign piece! Sometimes the game is successful. That explains theaters like The Contemporary and Theater on the Taganka. But most often, the actor fritters away his energies to no purpose on ephemeral and uninteresting roles.

The same thing happens in the cinema. Look what a solid reputation Vasily Shukshin seemed to have! However, he was allowed to do his own work "every other time"—one film, so to speak, on special order, the next one for himself. How he toiled over his *Stenka Razin!* Finally, they apparently approved the film, but again with a condition: that he first play Bondarchuk in the patriotic film—based on Sholokhov—*They Fought for Their Country,* and then... But the Soviet viewer will not see *Stenka Razin*—the fuss and nervous strain, the terrible, intense work undermined Vasily Shukshin's health, and he died during the filming.

XXII

In February 1966, the trial of the writers Sinyavsky and Daniel was to take place. During our career in literature, we have run into various forms of repression; but writers tried in a criminal court—that had never happened as far as we remembered! It was an obvious relapse of Stalinism, and we considered it our duty to protest. In general, as far as I know, several letters of protest against the sentencing of Sinyavsky and Daniel appeared, but our letter is the least known for some reason. Why? I believe the authorities deliberately kept it quiet because it was signed by the whole flower of young Soviet literature. Judge for yourself what signatures: Vasily Aksenov, Evgeny Evtushenko, Georgy Vladimov, Vladimir Voinovich, Boris Balter, Vasil Bykov, Bella Akhmadulina, Bulat Okudzhava, Yury Kazakov, Mikhail Roshchin, Vladimir Maximov—eighteen in all. We thought that Robert Rozhdestvensky would not sign, he'd already become an official figure—but Robert signed without hesitation. Then there was this extraordinary occurrence—I, for example, insisted categorically that the letter not even be shown to Andrei Voznesensky. The thing was, that Voznesensky had been nominated for the Lenin Prize for this narrative poem *Lonzhyumo,* and for Soviet writers, the Lenin Prize is election to the Immortals. But Andrei got wind of the letter anyway, sought us out himself, cursed us out and signed. He signed, understanding clearly that now he would never see a Lenin Prize.

By recalling once again the story of that letter, I am sure that I'm not putting the signers on the spot. In the first place, this "crime" must have been forgiven them according to the statute of limitations. Secondly, I believe my former colleagues are still of the opinion that a writer's work is not subject to consideration in a criminal court.

This was the last time our literary generation acted on a united front. From that moment, you can figure, our paths diverged. As one would expect, no letters of protest helped. Sinyavsky and Daniel got, respectively, seven and five years in hard-labor camps; and at a general meeting of Moscow writers, Sergei Mikhalkov declared (true, to cat-calls from the hall), "Lucky for us we've got the State Security Agencies." But Mikhalkov never makes a thoughtless or risky move, he always knows what to say and how. And in a very short time, Mikhalkov was appointed First Secretary of the Moscow Writers' Organization. As for the "signatories," various sanctions were applied against them. For example, the executive officer of the Central Committee officially announced to me:

> We are watching you carefully, and every one of your books raises a controversy, to put it mildly. Perhaps enough's enough? We advise you to translate.[1]

In short, each of us found out at his own cost that writing a letter to the Soviet government is a very risky affair. That's probably when this famous *chastushka* was composed:

To Klim Voroshilov,[2] I went to drop a line,
And then I thought it over and decided not to sign.

About a month later an event more comic than tragic occurred. A group of writers was arrested on Red Square, me among them. Here's what happened. There were rumors that on March 5, on the anniversary of Stalin's death, the old Bolsheviks were planning to hold a rally at the Mausoleum. It is still unclear where that news came from; perhaps it was simply a provocatory venture on the part of a certain agency, but we made no conjectures and decided not even to take part, but simply to see what would happen. After all, as the Soviet press writes, "Writers should be closer to life..."

And so, on the evening of March 5, several persons, including Vladimov, Yunna Morits, Arkady Arkanov, Aksenov and I, sinner that I am, set off straight from the House of Writers to Red Square. There were no old Bolsheviks at the Mausoleum, or young people either. However, you can't say the square was empty. Here and there stood tight little groups of middle-aged men who were looking at us with great curiosity. We knocked around awhile—seemed like there was no sign of a rally. I called one of my companions aside to the middle of the square, and then said, "Turn around..." Now, from the side, the picture was complete. Rogues in civvies lined the Kremlin walls, in different coats, it's true, but with the same fur hats, the kind worn only by employees of the Central Committee and the KGB. But one could scarcely suppose that all of a sudden all the Central Committee workers would en masse be dying for some fresh air. Which meant...

We returned to our guys and said, "Guys, there's nothing to do here. Let's go." We set off towards

[132]

GUM (one of us had to buy a watch), walking, of course, separately, in pairs; but at the doors of the store, anonymous civilians took each of us by the arm from behind, whispering in our ears, "Don't cause a fuss. You are under arrest. Let's get in the car."

We were taken, I think, to the fifteenth militia station, to the headquarters of the Komsomol *druzhina*[3] of the Komsomol Moscow City Committee. The professional civilians who arrested us did not appear again. But some young characters, real *druzhinniki*, kept looking into the room where we were left; and it struck us that there was such malevolence and hate in their looks that we might have been Japanese saboteurs at least. And yet these Komsomol members were probably our readers.

A man who introduced himself as the Third Secretary of the Komsomol City Committee called us out one by one to the "talks." I went first, since I supposed that my experience working in Komsomol papers would come in handy here. We chatted calmly, and I explained that apparently there had been some mistake—we were not some "bourgeois hirelings," but simple Soviet writers. It seemed to me that the Third Secretary was obviously disappointed, and he talked very briefly with my comrades, was interested basically in our papers, and even apologized to Aksenov. In two hours, they let us go, and the Komsomol *druzhinniki* no longer looked at us savagely.

The incident seemed settled. What's more, I repeat, they apologized to us. However, afterwards, every time I had to appear before the eyes of the higher level administration, the conversation invariably came round to the arrest on Red Square. Apparently that blot on my Soviet biography remained indelible.

A curious detail: nine years after that affair, one of

my comrades, a participant in the so-called demonstration, was speaking in the Great Hall of the Polytechnical Museum. When it was all over, a man completely unknown to him rushed up in the lobby and started going into raptures and, in general, talking as if to his best friend. It is, of course, always pleasant for a writer to talk with his admirers, but in this case, my friend began making tactless inquiries.

"Excuse me, but have we met?"

"Don't you remember?" asked the offended admirer. "I interrogated you after the arrest on Red Square! I was aiming high then, but later, like an idiot, I got the hots for some broad, and now I'm in the Znanie company. But the work's not tough. If you need a business trip somewhere—drop in, we'll set it up in a minute."

XXIII

Not long ago I went to Geneva and spoke to the students in the Russian department of the university there. My lecture was on contemporary Soviet literature, and I tried to speak objectively, noting all its pluses and minuses. The same day, they proposed I speak at an evening for fans of Russian letters. There is a circle in Geneva including undergraduates, graduate students at the university, translators working at UNESCO and simply Russians who long ago settled in Switzerland. But before the speech itself, I was warned that representatives of the first emigration would be coming, generally kind, benevolent people who, however, considered all the achievements of Russian literature in the last half-century tied with the names of writers who had emigrated. I was indignant. "How so? You mean they don't know Soviet literature!" And I got all wound up, as they say, and began to extol the virtues of Soviet literature, especially in the contemporary period, with such passion that an observer might have thought I was not an emigré writer but a propagandist sent by the ideological section of the Party Central Committee.

In my opinion this incident characterizes very precisely the psychology of the Soviet writer. In our own circle, we fulminate and find a mass of shortcomings in our prose and poetry; but when someone from outside attempts to strike out all of Soviet literature, we immediately become arrogant—one could scarcely find more zealous defenders.

In principle, on whatever side of the border they may be, patriotism has always been characteristic of real Soviet writers. And my literary generation was simply pro-Soviet by inclination. In our books we doggedly exposed the shortcomings of our Soviet reality, because we wanted to help our people build a happy life. We were convinced that one had to speak the truth to our people, only the truth, about both the past and the present. We believed that someday we would win the possibility of speaking forthrightly.

A strange paradox: writers live splendidly in our country, where they are to spit on the aspirations and needs of the people, and are preoccupied only with their own well-being. They have no problems at all. Today they're ordered to extol Stalin—they extol Stalin. Later they sing dithyrambs to "our Nikita Sergeevich," now they compose odes to "the wise and Party-spirited leadership and especially Leonid Ilych."[1] If tomorrow the papers were to say that Comrade Brezhnev himself was a spy for one of the imperialist intelligence organizations, the writers would begin in concert to fling mud at him. They will serve any sovereign "faithfully and true," because the authorities pay them generously to do so. And that's the sort of writers, if one may call them so, who are numbered in the ranks of true patriots in our country. And those writers who sincerely feel for the people and for the country, who boldly and openly expose shortcomings and receive only bumps and bruises in return—on those writers they pin the label "malicious carpers and rabid anti-Soviets."

However, the years pass and only these latter writers remain in the national memory, and only they are the pride of Soviet literature. Of course, in every period there was an official list of Soviet classics compiled, but some time later these inflated names would burst like soap bubbles, and their books would either be discarded from libraries as not wanted or still gather dust on the shelves. Yes, the real, truly patriotic, truly artistic books remained; but what a price their authors paid for their devotion, for the search for truth, and for their compromises with the authorities, for their voluntary or involuntary deals with their conscience There is nothing more tragic than the biographies of the Soviet writers whose names will enter the golden fund of Russian classics. Maxim Gorky, "stormy petrel of the Revolution," was horrified when he saw for himself what the Soviet regime had brought the people. With his forays in the press, Gorky attempted to rectify the situation; but just read what abuse they showered on the future founder of Socialist Realism in the Soviet papers beginning in 1918. Gorky emigrated and returned only at the end of the thirties, in general a broken man. But even this broken writer seemed dangerous to Stalin on the eve of the great purge, and he was poisoned. Alexei Tolstoi's best books were written in emigration. Mayakovsky shot himself. Esenin hanged himself. Pilnyak, Artem Vesely, Mandelstam, Babel were destroyed in the camps. Andrei Platonov died in poverty, Mikhail Bulgakov in obscurity. Some have fallen silent and stopped writing, like Vsevolod Ivanov, or taken to drink like Yury Olesha, or in the end committed suicide like Marina Tsvetaeva and Alexander Fadeev. Now books by Akhmatova, Zoshchenko, Pasternak are worth their weight in gold, but we remember what a terrible steamroller ran over them in the lamentably famous Party resolutions! We remember what badgering Ehrenburg and Tvardovsky endured. What literature, what other country can boast such a sad martyrology!

[137]

In our liberal times, writers are not shot. But look who turned up in emigration—Solzhenitsyn, Joseph Brodsky,, Sasha Sokolov, Natalia Gorbanevskaya, Sinyavsky, Viktor Nekrasov and Vladimir Maximov, Naum Korzhavin and Alexander Galich—the best representatives of Russian letters! And how many other writers reached for the bitter bread abroad: Anatoly Kuznetsov, Meros, Maramzin, Svirsky, Belinkov... Because of the good life they led there or what? Voinovich, Vladimov, Kornilov have been or are on the verge of being expelled from the Union of Writers. True, now such great names of our generation as Akhmadulina, Aksenov, Bitov, Evtushenko, Kazakov, Konetsky, Okudzhava, Rozhdestvensky, Voznesensky, are in *The Great Soviet Encyclopedia*—that is, they have at last been recognized—but again we recall how, not so long ago, the splintery critical cudgel worked them over.

If you believe the current official literary scholarship, we are obliged to the Soviet regime for all our successes in Soviet literature. Well, there were, of course, some writers who made some mistakes, but basically it was thanks to wise Party policy and the administration's support of the creative unions that these writers achieved such profundity in their work. Absolutely not! Not thanks to, but *despite*! The best books appeared despite the authorities. And if Soviet literature has really made a contribution to world culture, it is because Russia is rich in talent—you can't put everyone in jail, you can't shut everyone's mouth. Like our glorious forefathers, the Russian writers of the nineteenth century, honest Soviet writers have served not the powers that be, but their people.

XXIV

Yes, in our liberal times, they don't shoot writers. They try to buy them off or shut them up. But when a writer's mouth is shut for him, he either, as Mayakovsky says, "stands on the throat of his own song,"[1] or there are consequences just as tragic. In this connection, the fate of two writers whom I knew rather well is instructive.

Boris Balter was sixteen years older than I. A participant in the Fatherland War, a front-line officer, battalion commander, he was severely wounded at the front. His literary career took shape with difficulty—the thing was that his name was Jewish, Boris Isaakovich, and the last name was suspicious too—Balter, and *that* during the period of struggle with international Zionism. In short, he entered big-time literature only in 1962, with the publication of the novella *Goodbye, Boys!* in *Youth* magazine. Therefore, I boldly reckon him among writers of my literary generation. *Goodbye, Boys!* was a great success among the readers; there was a film based on the novella; in 1965, in the same magazine, he published a second novella, *In Transit*; and later... And later he signed a letter in defense of Sinyavsky and Daniel, and then a second letter in defense of Galanskov and Ginzberg. Boris Balter was expelled from the Party and ceased to be published. His earlier services were forgotten; no one considered that a literary talent had perished

—they were just following instructions from above.

In order to earn his bread, Balter was forced to translate from Uzbek and Tadzhik, to write screenplays on other people's books for film studios in the Central Asian republics. In short, to be a literary day-laborer.

You can understand his mental condition. A man with a real name in literature is forced to ask for unskilled work from minor literary bureaucrats, to feel himself constantly humiliated and constantly to recognize that the path to the reader is closed to him forever. Can one stand such a life for long? Boris Balter died in 1974 of a broken heart.

I ran over to *The Literary Gazette* and asked to submit an obituary. "Why take vengeance on a dead writer?" I asked. "He's no longer dangerous to the authorities!" The employees who knew me sighed sympathetically, but they all agreed that there must be instructions on it from the Secretariat of the Moscow Writers' Organization. At the Moscow organization, the new secretary, a man said to be liberal-minded, treated my request with understanding. He quickly started calling up *The Literary Gazette*, but when he got through to the first assistant editor, his tone immediately changed—apparently he was given the appropriate explanations: Balter did not deserve an obituary in a central paper. However, the secretary pushed through permission for an obituary in a smaller-scale paper—*Literary Russia*. "So write an obituary," the secretary said to me.

They brought me Boris Balter's personal file from the archive. In it, all of the writer's sins were scrupulously recorded, but not a word of the success his books enjoyed. Two hours later I laid the finished obituary on the secretary's desk. The secretary read through it, and again sighed. "Old man, if you want the obituary to see the light of day, we'll have to scratch all of this."

[140]

And he scratched out any good words I had to say. But to the newspaper editor even the bare biographical information seemed "unfitting" for Balter. A few lines appeared in the paper: "With deep regret we announce . . . and express our condolences to. . ." Friends tried to get a reissue of Boris Balter's old stories through the publishers—but the publishers are still delaying their answer. That is all. It is as if no such writer had ever existed in our country.

Another career. The poet and script-writer Gennady Shpalikov. He achieved notoriety as the author of the scenario for the film *Ilich's Barrier*. But when "high government criticism" came down on the film, Gena lost heart and instantly wrote the scenario for another film *Wandering through Moscow*. This film the critics greeted favorably. Some guys walk around Moscow, sing, meet some girls, are ready to go through "tundra and taiga," and most important—they do not think about anything serious. Now that's how it should be, those are "real representatives of the younger generation..." Shpalikov continued to write scenarios in the same vein, avoiding sharp angles, and outwardly his career was turning out well. Films came out, there was fame and money. What else does a man need? But Shpalikov had other works too; he tried not to show them, understanding that it was senseless. The country sang his songs: "Oh you riggings, riggings," "Indian Summer,"... But connoisseurs of *samizdat*[2] would quote his verses on the Tsar-bell.[3] In this poem, some speculator sold the Tsar-bell to the British ambassador, and then:

> Triumph and rejoicing there was in the West,
> And from the bell they stamped out bronze
> buttons for their vests.

In chains the speculator set off for
                    Taishet's waste;
We made ourselves another bell of card-
                    board, glue and paste.
We hid disgrace and infamy, had no
                    fear of the Lord;
And deeply moved beside the gun—
                    Rabindranath Tagore.[4]
He walked around and all about and
                    gave the side a tap,
About our bell, in any case, he
                    never made a crack.

Having made a deal with his own conscience, Shpalikov felt a spiritual discord. And in the bitter Russian tradition, he tried to drown his sorrow in wine. He drank more and more. On November 1, 1974, Gennady Shpalikov hanged himself in his room at the Union of Writers House of Creation in Peredelkino. I repeat, outwardly his affairs were going well. That very day they had called from Mosfilm to tell him they were offering him a new contract. That is why the managers of the House of Creation had knocked so persistently at his door, though they got no answer. They called the militia, drew up a statement. It turned out that in accordance with some strange instructions, the militia did not take "county suicides" to the morgue. With one of my friends I had to accompany Shpalikov's body to Moscow. We brought his body to the Moscow Morgue on Shukin Street late in the evening. The receptionist took the papers through the window and then allowed me to come into the office alone. My friend was not allowed in. "It's so terrifying!" the female attendant complained. "A maniac is going around the city robbing and killing women!..."

"Why should you be afraid," I asked, surprised, "you aren't working in a savings bank!"

"I'm afraid of men anyway," said the attendant and started to fill out the papers. On the dirty, badly plastered wall hung a vivid poster: "We'll make Moscow the model Communist city!—L.I. Brezhnev."

"And now, go into the basement and get the stretcher," said the attendant. My friend and I went down into the basement, I grabbed the stretcher and automatically jerked back my hand—the stretcher was smeared with blood. "We don't have any others," the attendant remarked maliciously.

We laid Shpalikov on the stretcher, carried him down to the basement, closed the door. Such was the last trip of that talented writer.

And a third career. Kostya Bogatyrev was killed right after my departure from the Soviet Union. He was supposedly killed by drunks in the entranceway of the writers' housing cooperative. But I know these Aeroport apartment buildings very well. The liftladies[5] are on duty around the clock; there were practically never any brawls. This was in a restricted apartment block, not some Marina Grove.[6] And Konstantin Bogatyrev, a brilliant translator of German, was a real intellectual, not a drunken bully. Whom could he have crossed? Who had a personal score to settle with him? Only those who did not like the fact that he signed letters in defense of political prisoners, that he handed these letters over to foreign correspondents, that he often visited Academician Sakharov. So they got him out of the way.

XXV

Once, still during my studies at the Literary Institute, I ran over to my friend's, an upperclassman (I won't give his name, he is now of very high rank). So, I ran over to his place early in the morning and got him out of bed.

"Listen," I said, "I didn't sleep at all last night, just thought—and you know what conclusion I came to? There is no such thing as Socialist Realism! It's all a fraud, a swindle, and simply a rehash of medieval romanticism..."

I was long expounding my ideas on this matter, and my friend looked at me as if I were an idiot and then burst out laughing. "What, you only just figured that out now?"

Really, it is funny now to recall what nonsense they beat into our heads! Each of us had to invent the alphabet on his own, and each agonizingly freed himself of naive illusions.

Our most widespread illusion was precisely formulated by the author of the anonymous revolutionary pamphlet that appeared more than one hundred years ago, after the reforms of Alexander II.[1] Remember that famous line "For how many centuries has Rus been ruined by faith in the Tsar's good intentions!" Precisely so: closing our eyes to the obvious facts, we have continued to believe in the good intentions of the authorities, or at least to believe that those intentions would someday materialize. Everything, or almost everything, I have said in these notes I tried to say in Moscow from the podium at meetings (if I was given the opportunity) or in private semiofficial conversations with the administration (if the administration called me up for their usual reprimand). And every time, I only managed to convince the administration of my "unreliability." It is curious that when we touched on the general state of literature, the administration would clearly start to get bored and try to change the topic of conversation. At best I'd be offered a free pass to the House of Creation.

But how many sleepless nights did I orate and, smoking one cigarette after another, try to convince my invisible interlocutor that a situation in literature like the current one was impossible, and would end with the best writers going abroad and the best books being published overseas. My presumed interlocutor changed each time. This one, I thought, understands it all himself, but can't do a thing. Contrariwise, it is to that one's advantage that exceptional manuscripts not be published—for only against a background of general dullness could he look like any sort of writer. This one could care less about anything in general; he wants a high position and nothing is of interest to him besides his own career; and he knows perfectly well that by supporting "disgraced writers" you'll only wring your own neck. But there must be a man who is not indifferent to the fate of the literature of the Fatherland! There must be a master in Russia! And with this "master of Russia" I conducted heated night-time arguments. "Well fine," I said, "I understand how busy you are with relations with China, the munitions industry, and the eternal problems with agriculture. You personally do not need

[145]

an honest Soviet literature, it only causes you anxiety. But even to surpass America in class and quality of rockets, you need engineers, physicists, mathematicians, and the technical intelligentsia cannot be content with just academic soldering and their rations. They need spiritual sustenance! You know very well that the technical intelligentsia does not eat Sofronovs and Kochetovs, they need our books because they find in them a reflection of their own ideas. Even if we make a lot of mistakes, we are still interested in the State. If our books are not published, there will be a vacuum; and there cannot be a vacuum. That means, instead of our books, they'll read foreign ones by quite unfriendly authors, etc., etc." That is the spirit in which I harangued myself, very convincingly, it seemed to me then.

But no, I never chanced to chat with the "master of Russia" personally. Perhaps there isn't one? Some are preoccupied only with getting a higher position, others with holding onto it somehow. Industry is still operating at a loss; and though the sixtieth year of the Soviet regime has already passed, there is nothing to feed the people, and it is necessary to buy grain from America. When is one to think of the fate of belles-lettres? In the last forty years it has become a tradition in our country for executive positions in the field of literature to be sinecures for failures, for failures, naturally, from the ranks of Party functionaries. This one couldn't cope with the chemical industry, that one mucked up agriculture, a third disgraced himself in the United Nations... Where do you stick such people? Still, they've got *nomenklatura*. Ah, let them go manage literature and art!

In his time, when Molotov was more powerful than Malenkov, and Malenkov had displeased the Chairman of the Soviet of Peoples' Commissars, Molotov threatened

Georgy Maximilianovich, "I'll appoint you People's Commissar of Culture, and that'll teach you!"

Become merely the People's Commissar of Culture? Truly a frightful prospect. You can't fall any lower!

Recently the Soviet newspapers published a Central Committee resolution on work with the creative cadres. Many things were correctly noted. There really is no fresh supply of creative powers; the youth really is being kept down. But we are used to getting periodic resolutions from the Central Committee almost every week—on work at the bath and laundry centers, or on the chemical industry. That is the administration's style now—adopt a resolution. So the papers will make a fuss on the assigned theme for two weeks or so—then, unfortunately, everything will be as it was before. To radically change the situation in literature, you would at least have to change the administration in the publishing houses and magazines. But the Kozhevnikovs, Alexeevs, Lesyuchevskys and Sofronovs sit firmly in their editors' and directors' chairs. Will these talentless writers and arch-politicians really fight against dullness in literature? Will these suppressors of everything new and talented really foster gifted youth? I hope they forgive my uncouth comparison, but while goats are tending the garden, there's no sense expecting a good cabbage harvest!

We were young twenty years ago. So where is the new literary generation? There are individual good poems, there are individual good stories, but there's no new generation. As Andrei Voznesensky noted in his article in *The Literary Gazette*, "the new generation has not yet crystallized." Why? For the very reasons I spoke of.

In regard to literature, the Party has always adhered to a policy of "lash and gingerbread." Faithful servants of the Party receive not just gingerbread, but gingerbread houses. In the whole world you won't find writers who, with minimal effort, could have such an easy life.

The lash hangs as before above the heads of the recalcitrant and disobedient. The lash is silence in the press about your earlier published works (they finally understood that abuse for ideological mistakes only brings popularity); the lash is when your books are scratched from publication plans, and the editor-in-chief of the magazine in which you are usually printed throws up his hands, averts his eyes and whispers something like "Of course, I'd be glad to...personally I like it...but you see for yourself, it's impossible just now"; the lash is when you feel yourself scratched from literature in general—there was no such writer, there is not and there shall not be! And finally, the lash is the real threat of expulsion from the Union of Writers, and then you are deprived not only of all professional income, but of the possibility of getting any sort of work (they won't even take you in a bakery now—"but you're a writer, you have a higher education, we can't take you").

However, in my opinion, the current situation in our literature is unusual in that they're starting to pass out gingerbread to certain recalcitrant writers (although, as Bulat Okudzhava's song says, there isn't enough gingerbread to go around). What's more, individual writers whom they haven't yet managed to buy, and who stand on the threshold of "dissidence," are suddenly shown a big piece of cake under the table.

How is this done? I shall give an example from my own experience.

Two years ago, the board of Mosfilm studios asked me to write a scenario on Felix Dzherzhinsky.[2] I should say that for a long period before this I had been earning my bread with house reviews for magazines (slave labor) and my relations with the publishers remained, if not disputatious, at least undefined. And suddenly—this honor.

Naturally, I'm interested in where the idea came from. They explain politely that the director of the film is in love with my *Robespierre* (my novel *The Gospel According to Robespierre* came out in 1970), and won't hear of any other author. That would be normal, the director is the boss in the cinema. But when I talk with the director face-to-face, it turns out that he never read a single line of my work. I probably seem an idiot to the director, for he casts all diplomacy aside and lays his cards on the table:

"Anatoly Tikhonovich! Maybe one part isn't enough for you? All right, it'll be two. If you want, it'll be five. If you want, it'll be a joint Soviet-Polish production, you'll go to Poland on business.[3] Five parts! You know what kind of money that is? I was guaranteed that the studio would accept any terms."

Of course, he had in mind financial terms. And he was not deceiving me, he had been guaranteed. But the question was—by whom? Alas, he preferred not to enlarge on that theme.

But why, why did the wind suddenly change? Why, despite the fact that I had not changed, and what's more, had spoken sharply at some meetings (when I managed to get through to the podium), did three publishing houses in 1975 alone publish three of my books (of course, after cutting them up pretty weell, there being no other way). But they published three of my books! Why did they suddenly let Aksenov and O-kudzhava go abroad? Why, when Voinovich was virtually expelled from the Union of Writers, did they

[149]

phone him up from the secretariat of the Moscow organization and, purling tenderly into the receiver, offer to forget all old grudges and let him return to the maternal bosom? Why did they drag out Kornilov's expulsion from the Union of Writers for so long? And finally, they clearly intended to chuck Vladimov out of the organization for his *True Ruslan*, but no, a sharp about-face—and there's an interview with Vladimov on the front page of *The Literary Gazette*; and at Contemporary Publishers, Vladimov's long-suffering novel *Three Minutes of Silence* is put on the typesetting schedule... I won't even speak of Yury Trifonov. After receiving the Stalin Prize at the beginning of his career, he was virtually silent for many long years, but recently reappeared to the Soviet reader as a qualitatively new writer. One after another his novellas come out—*The Exchange, The Long Goodbye, Taking Stock, Impatience, Another Life*. True, there was a rumor that Comrade Suslov[4] himself "was pleased to express dissatisfaction" with the novel *Impatience.* Clouds started to gather over Trifonov, but the thunder never rumbled, and in the January 1976 issue of *Peoples' Friendship* magazine they published Trifonov's novella *The House on the Embankment*—and the reading public struck its brow in bewilderment: how did they let that through?

Miracles, simply! But we, trained in Marxist ideology, understood perfectly well that miracles do not happen. If our government could fence off the USSR from the whole world with a Great Wall, then of course they wouldn't stand on ceremony with the writers, and the writers I mentioned wouldn't be sunning themselves on Koktebel beaches, and certainly wouldn't be junketing abroad—they would be sucking their thumbs somewhere around Vorkuta.[5] But the whole thing is that

[150]

once again (for the nth time), the nation of triumphant socialism cannot make ends meet in its economy and is asking for help from the capitalists. But in order to negotiate and beg for credit, the regime must for the sake of propriety array itself in civilian garb. How? It couldn't take its tanks out of Eastern Europe or dismantle its intercontinental missiles. Another solution is found: the regime immediately puts on the bright vest of a supposedly free literature and hopes that now the USSR will pass for a completely democratic state, so that there will be other chances to wrap the "accursed West" (for the nth time!) around its little finger. In sum, it is time to understand that the real basis of all the cultural "miracles" in Russian life that inhabitants of Europe and America goggle at dumbfoundedly is economic dependence on the West. If one fine morning, in the twinkling of an eye, Communism reigned over the whole country, by evening Sofia Vlasievna would have gobbled up all the recalcitrants with great appetite and wouldn't even spit out the buttons. That's first.

Second. However strange it may seem, for now, it is useful for the authorities to have in reserve a few well-known disobedient writers so that, if worst comes to worst, they can be made scapegoats at the next failure in industry or agriculture. By the way, the Jews come in handy here too. We've seen that, and more than once.

Third. Carried away by their own tricks with détente and de-escalation, the regime has made a few blunders. Now Soviet writers have the possibility of more or less quietly emigrating. In the past that wasn't the case. The writer was confronted with a choice—they either broke him or bought him. No third choice was offered. But then Solzhenitsyn left, Brodsky left, Maximov left, and to the horror of the authorities, not only did they not die of hunger next to the fence, but on the contrary, developed to the full height of their talents. Now the writer in Russia, driven to extremes, doesn't soap the noose in grief; he feverishly tries to remember if he has among his kin even distant European relatives! And for this reason—oh, how difficult it has become for the Party administration to work with the writers! The administration, in true Soviet fashion, in true Party fashion, according to the principle of push comes to shove, just wants to put a bullet between the recalcitrant's eyes, but there's an order from above: "Don't, they'll scatter!"

"But he lacks ideological content! He's an ideological saboteur! He writes this, says that! He doesn't recognize the authorities!" groans the offended administration.

In answer: "We know nothing about that. But you were appointed to work with him!"

The administration cries and sobs, swallows "tears the world sees not," wipes its eyes (oh, if this were Tula or Tambov, we'd stifle him on the quiet, but in Moscow you can't, there'll be a stink), and the administration has to smile happily at the disobedient writer and offer him a modest assortment of gingerbread.

But I don't feel like sorting out the events of the last few years in detail. Who knows, my comments might prevent a writer from publishing a book, or indiscreet praise will provoke a shower of repression against my former comrade... Our paths have diverged; my comrades stayed in Russia and I would like to wish them courage, patience, good humor, and, as I often said at our common board, "success in public, private and family life."

The generation in which the new literature was born has in principle been obliged to be profoundly pro-Soviet. After all, it grew up with a new Russia. So it is all the more significant that opponents of the regime turned up in that generation too. But even those writers who became defenders of the regime reflect objective reality. For example, I described how even the successful poet Robert Rozhdestvensky gradually became official. Did he lose popularity? Completely—with one section of the public; but then he gained another, a mass audience. I recall that we joked in Moscow that nowadays all the songs are to Robert's words. And he has lots of admirers; they're the same people who regard the Soviet system as a streetcar—the important thing for them is to hop in the car and get the best seat possible. And you don't have to do anything else. The streetcar moves by itself. Really, just try to find another country in the world where everyone seems to be working and at the same time no one *is* working. And why should you take the trouble? The streetcar is carrying you, you don't have to get a place up front and stick out. And why think? Let the authorities think, they get paid a lot. Especially since the streetcar passengers have one unspoken privilege now: they can curse the authorities as much as they please (in a whisper, don't stick out!). Now it is permitted. The streetcar driver pretends he doesn't hear a thing. Well, of course, at stops (meetings) everyone is obliged to recite slogans, as fare for the ride. Pretty cheap. The price of a slogan, like a tram ticket, is three kopeks.

So what do we remember when we're nostalgic? Of course, not the monuments to leaders in the central squares of Russian cities. But we do remember our friends, our nearest and dearest, we remember the best years of our lives (of our youth), and we remember songs, books, poems, plays and films with our wonderful actors... And it just occurred to me—doesn't the creative intelligentsia's fault lie in the fact that its work made the Soviet system more attractive? Imagine what it would have been like if only the talentless had collaborated with the authorities. How dreary the spiritual life of Russia would have looked! Brezhnev's speeches, Central Committee resolutions, Oshanin's verse, Sofronov's plays... Why you would hang yourself from boredom! And perhaps the passengers on the tram would have revolted out of tedium and ennui.

So who outplayed whom? The government or the writers?

My colleagues' books, like my own, entered Soviet Russian culture. Thanks to them, the crafty regime makes the governmental system more attractive. And even the fact that there are lots of caustic hints, ironic associations, criticisms in the books—all the same, the regime can put all of that to its own use now: "see what freedoms are permitted in our country!" So, to sum up, can one say that, alas, the Soviet of Deputies was simply using us?

So who won the duel,
Martynov or Lermontov?[1]

The question would seem clear, historically demonstrable, and nevertheless new generations, along with the author of those lines, Bella Akhmadulina, continue to try to find out—who was it won?

In the beginning of my book, I explained that I had emigrated. The new emigration, like one of the first Russian emigré writers, Alexander Herzen,[2] is awakening Russia, ringing not the little streetcar bell, but the bell of Russian freedom. But will many hear us at home? Let it be only a few, but they shall hear! One must strike the bell!

NOTES

I

1. *The Literary Gazette*, weekly literary newspaper published by the Union of Writers of the USSR.

2. *Detgiz*, Children's Literature State publishing house, the largest publisher of children's books in the Soviet Union.

3. *Oprichina*, the private household created by Ivan the Terrible (1565) to administer those Russian lands that had been confiscated and placed under the Tsar's direct control.

4. Moscow's House of Writers, in the huge neo-classical mansion of the Dolgoruky family, contains an excellent restaurant.

5. Sofia Vlasievna, name and patronymic used ironically in reference to *sovetskaya vlast'* ("Soviet regime," "Soviet power").

6. Official graphomaniacs.

7. From the lyric poem "My Comrades" (1963).

II

1. Fadeev's *The Young Guard* (1945) concerns the activities of an underground group of Komsomol members during the German occupation. It was enthusiastically received by Soviet critics, but later criticized for minimizing the role of the Party leadership. Fadeev was forced to revise the novel in 1951. He later committed suicide.

2. Gladilin hints that Sholokhov's long novel *Virgin Soil Upturned* (part one published 1931) is much inferior to *The Quiet Don* (1928-33, 1940). There were persistent rumors that Sholokhov was not the author of the latter work, that it was written by a White Army officer on whose body the manuscript was found, and that Sholokhov appropriated the novel.

3. First All-Union Congress of Soviet Writers (1934).

4. A wave of antisemitism, thinly disguised as a campaign against "rootless cosmopolitans." The attacks on Akhmatova and Zoshchenko, as well as those who would "worship at the shrine of bourgeois-philistine culture," appeared in a resolution passed by the Central Committee of the Communist Party on August 14, 1946. See *The Central Committee Resolution and Zhdanov's Speech on the Journals* Zvezda *and* Leningrad, tr. Felicity Ashbee and Irina Tidmarsh (Detroit: Strathcona, 1978), bilingual edition.

5. Pavel Korchagin, ideal Soviet youth, hero of Nikolai Ostrovsky's novel *How the Steel was Tempered* (1935).

6. Pavlik Morozov (1918-32), young pioneer and Soviet martyr in the struggle for collectivization. His name is the first inscribed in the Honor Roll of the All-Union Pioneer Organization.

7. I.e., in restricted areas.

8. Dostoevsky was essentially unpublished in the Soviet Union from 1930 until 1956.

9. The Lenin Library in central Moscow is one of the largest public research libraries in the world.

10. I.e., after Malenkov's fall from grace in 1957, following his participation in the "anti-Party group's" unsuccessful effort to depose Krushchev.

11. Communal apartments, still common in Moscow and Leningrad, consist of three or four rooms, each housing one family unit, and a common kitchen, bathroom and toilet. Privacy, for which there is no word in

Russian, is at a minimum.

12. Well-orchestrated "spontaneous" displays of patriotism by remarkably unenthusiastic workers, soldiers and students on the anniversaries of the October Revolution and Comintern Day, respectively.

13. Popular soccer teams. The Central Club of the Red Army (CCRA) has a team that occupies a position analogous to Annapolis or West Point in American football. Dynamo is the team of the police and KGB.

14. Soviet newspapers normally contain only four pages. The first two report on government and Party activity, progress in agriculture and industry, and local workers' initiatives and achievements. The third page is devoted to international news, the fourth to sports. Speeches and documents are quoted in full; accidents and natural disasters within the USSR are omitted as "untypical."

15. Urban high schools became coeducational only during the reforms of 1956-58.

16. Headquarters of the syndicates of the USSR, formerly the Club of the Nobility (1785). In the Column Hall, the most elegant room in Moscow, both Lenin and Stalin lay in state.

17. *Druzhinniki*, members of the voluntary vigilante patrol organized in 1958 to assist the police in combatting hooliganism, drunkenness, littering and jaywalking.

18. Workdays, the units of payment on collective farms (*kolkhozy*), which are organized on factory lines.

19. *Stilyagi*, young people excessively concerned with fashionable clothes and Western jazz.

20. Alleged conspiracy of prominent Soviet medical specialists to murder leading government and Party officials (1953).

21. Chapter Four of the *Short Course in the History of the CPSU* contained the quintessence of Marxist creed and was written by Stalin himself. While its author lived, the *Short Course* was the bedside book of every literate Soviet citizen.

III

1. The large Soviet car is a symbol of class and status.

IV

1. Russian city in the Altai Territory, near the Soviet-Mongol border.

2. The literary almanac (Vol. 1, 1955; Vol. 2, 1956) included works by writers previously proscribed, several stories dealing with Soviet life in the spirit of critical realism, and some daring essays.

3. Kuznetsov later defected, changed his name, and denounced the published versions of his books.

4. Alexander Tvardovsky, who had been editor of *New World* previously (1950-54), succeeded Konstantin Simonov in 1958. He retained the editorship until shortly before his death in 1971.

5. A major automotive industrial city in central Russia, northeast of Moscow.

V

1. In the marking system used in Russian educational institutions, the highest grade is a "five."

2. There was a major currency reform in 1958, the new ruble equalling ten old rubles. Graduate students currently receive a stipend of 70-80 rubles a month, undergraduates, 35-40, compared with the monthly salary of a young "member of the technical intelligentsia" of around 110 rubles. Students normally live at home or in rent-free dormitories, and often receive considerable assistance from their families to get by on what amounts to a very tight food and entertainment allowance.

3. A trip to the baths costs all of 15-20 kopeks, 10 kopeks extra for soap. The baths are a major form of entertainment for many Soviets, who spend hours scrubbing, soaping and steaming with their buddies between breaks for vodka, beer and smoked fish in the dressing room.

4. Russian students call each other by first names. Use of name and patronymic is a mark of respect normally reserved for one's elders or superiors.

5. When Krushchev opened up the campaign against Stalin and abuses in the past.

VI

1. The magazine officially adopted the Tyumen project. Such sponsorship (*shefstvo*) may involve cultural or educational help to isolated regions or a sort of sister-project exchange of information. In this case, of course, the magazine staff is expected to write (as well as learn) about their comrades at the showcase Tyumen project.

2. Since meat, fruit and fresh vegetables are in chronically short supply, high-ranking Soviets have the privilege of ordering food from well-stocked warehouses through their employer or their professional union.

3. Iosif Stalin's patronymic.

4. The most official official writer, author of the words to the Soviet National Anthem, etc.

VII

No notes to this section.

VIII

1. *Nomenklatura*. A: list of posts in State institutions to which appointments are made by Party committees. B: list of persons whom the Party considers eligible for such appointments. C: table establishing equivalence of rank in different hierarchies.

2. Actors, artists and musicians in the Soviet Union are awarded honorific titles by their national republics and by the State which are regularly used in programs, film credits and periodicals. The two grades are *zasluzhennyi* ("honored") and the more prestigious *narodnyi* ("national") artist.

[161]

IX

1. Moscow Art Theatre, the famous repertory group founded in 1898 by Stanislavsky and Nemirovich-Danchenko, and closely associated with Anton Chekhov, whose works it first staged, and later with Maxim Gorky.

2. All-Union State Cinematography Institute.

X

1. Pushkin's *Eugene Onegin* VIII. 13. 1-2.

2. Bratsk Hydro-Electric Power Station. Show project of the early 1960s and title of a collection of poems by Evtushenko (1965).

3. The Kolyma upland along the northeastern shore of the Sea of Okhotsk is an important gold-mining region administered from the port of Magadan.

4. Councils on National Economy, regional economic management boards abolished in 1965 in favor of tighter central control.

5. Chukotka, easternmost peninsula of Siberia.

6. MAZ, a truck produced by the Minsk Motor Vehicle Factory.

7. Omul, a fish of the salmon family. Yaranga, a portable home among peoples of eastern Siberia.

XI

1. Stalin Prizes were granted annually between 1941 and 1952 for achievement in literature (prose fiction, poetry and drama), art and labor.

2. Perekop, which connects the Crimea to the mainland, was the site of innumerable battles, among them the final defeat of the anti-Bolshevik forces led by Baron Wrangel in November 1920. Magnitogorsk is the showcase building site of the metallurgical industrial complex (built 1929-31) in the southern foothills of the Urals.

XII

1. *Serpastyi, molotkastyi*, neologisms from Mayakovsky's "Poem on My Soviet Passport" (1929).

2. "Thank you very much" in Russian, with stress transposed in both words from the second to the last syllable, where it is fixed in French.

3. A two-line, rhymed, accentual verse form that easily lends itself to witty, and usually obscene, improvisations at drinking parties.

4. Since rubles have no value outside the Soviet Union, the State provides Soviet tourists abroad with a small per diem allowance in the "hard currency" of the country they are visiting. To save the country's foreign currency reserves, nearly all expenses are planned in advance, calculated as part of the package tour, and paid for in kind through Intourist.

XIII

1. From Pushkin's mock-romantic ballad *Ruslan and Lyudmila* (1817-20), canto I, 11, 1-2.

2. Lev Nikolaevich Oshanin (b. 1912), Russian poet of the romance of love and construction.
3. Krushchev's first name and patronymic.

XIV

1. Old Bolsheviks and Red Army officers during the Civil War. They were liquidated by Stalin in the Purge of 1934-38.
2. The poem, which deals with Russian antisemitism, appeared September 19, 1961. The title refers to a ravine outside Kiev where thousands of Jews, gypsies and Slavs were executed by the Nazis.
3. A reference to Voznesensky's poem "Parabolic Ballad" (1959).
4. Trans-sense or transrational language (*zaum*) was a contribution of the Futurists.

XV

1. Lajos Kossuth (1802-94), symbol of revolutionary nationalism. His brief period of power in the revolutionary years of 1848 and 1849 was ended by Russian armies.
2. Lev Tolstoi's family estate.

XVI

1. Soviet libraries virtually all have closed stacks, but the reference here is to the innumerable special collections (*spetsialnye khranilishcha*) that restrict access to all but the currently acceptable Soviet publications.
2. This "young prose" is described and discussed in Priscilla Meyer, "Aksenov and the Soviet Literature of the 1960s," RLT, No. 6 (Spring 1973), pp. 447-60.
3. Pankin is currently the chief officer of the Soviet copyright agency—sole agent for all Soviet writers whose works can appear in translation.
4. Russian literary journals, often several hundred pages an issue, include sections of prose fiction, poetry, journalism, literary criticism, short book reviews, and articles on art and music.

XVII

1. The Riding School (Manège) near the Kremlin was built in 1817 and fitted out as a large exhibition hall in 1958.
2. Burying place of many famous Russians, outside the walls of the sixteenth-century Novodevichi Monastery.
3. Neizvestny emigrated to the United States in 1977.
4. Russian epic songs dealing with legendary folk heroes and the history of ancient Rus.
5. Alexander Kolchak (1874-1920), Russian admiral and leader of the anti-Bolshevik forces in the Far East during the civil war. Anton Denikin (1872-1947), supreme commander of the White armies (1918-20), led the anti-Bolshevik forces in southern Russia.

XVIII

1. Member of the Party or government machine.
2. Originally called the Third Studio, the company was renamed for the actor and director Evgeny Vakhtangov (1883-1922) who managed it from 1920 and produced some of the most original productions of post-Revolutionary theater.
3. *Zaveduyushchii literatury*, head of the literary department in Soviet theaters.
4. Cured fillet of sturgeon.
5. Hotel facilities administered by the artistic unions for artists and writers.
6. English translation in V. Aksenov, *The Steel Bird and Other Stories* (Ann Arbor: Ardis, 1979).

XIX

1. Housing-Utilization Office.
2. Moscow Organization of Soviet Artists.
3. An extensive agricultural development project in the steppes of Kazakhstan and western Siberia begun in 1954, diverting men and resources from cultivated lands.

XX

1. Gladilin's name and the prefixed verb used both come from the root *glad-* ("smooth"), with connotations of ironing and verbal facility. The gladilinian novel was to be further gladilized.
2. *Fourth Prose* (1930 or 1931, first published 1966), section 2. See Jane Gary Harris (ed.), Osip Mandelstam, *The Complete Critical Prose and Letters* (Ann Arbor: Ardis, 1979), pp. 312-29.
3. Alexei Gavrilovich Venetsianov (1780-1847), painter whose subjects included idealized portraits of peasants and idyllic scenes of village life. His students were of more naturalistic tendency.
4. Agitation and propaganda section of central and local committees of the CPSU.
5. *Valyuta* is any hard currency traded in Western markets. The ruble is a soft currency, officially unexportable and without value outside the USSR. The privileged classes in the Soviet Union receive part of their salary in "certificates" (*valyuta* in ruble denominations), negotiable only in special stores offering foreign imports (from herring to stereo equipment) purchased with the state's limited supply of foreign currency, as well as Soviet products manufactured exclusively for sale abroad. Certificates sell for about eight times their face value on the black market.

XXI

1. A young engineer or doctor—to pick other "intellectual workers"—makes about 120 rubles.
2. A multiple enterprise consisting of shoe and appliance repair, laundry and dry-cleaning service, haircutting, etc.
3. The ubiquitous radios with which such institutions are provided

have only one knob—a volume control, so they receive only one station and are on unless unplugged.

4. The department of the Ministry of Culture dealing with the theater.

5. The *CheKa* (Extraordinary Commission for combatting counter-revolution, sabotage and speculation) was the name of the Soviet security agency from 1918 to 1922.

XXII

1. Translation is the traditional path of Russian writers eager to publish, earn money and yet avoid the vagaries of government censors—tsarist or Soviet. The writer has considerable leeway translating from obscure Turkic or Finno-Ugric languages of which the censor—and often the "translator"—have no knowledge.

2. Kliment Efremovich Voroshilov (1881-1969). At this time Voroshilov was presidium chairman of the Supreme Soviet and a member of the presidium of the Party Central Committee.

3. In the USSR, the militia is a civil force corresponding to the police in other countries. The voluntary people's *druzhina* ("patrol") assists the militia.

XXIII

1. Brezhnev's name and patronymic.

XXIV

1. From the poem "A Cloud in Trousers" (1915).

2. Works independently "published," i.e., laboriously retyped and passed on to friends.

3. The heaviest bell in the world (c. 465,000 pounds), cast in 1733-35, it stands on a pedestal in the Kremlin.

4. Rabindranath Tagore (1861-1941), Bengali poet, novelist, essayist and political leader, awarded the Nobel Prize for literature in 1913. He traveled widely in Europe, Asia and America in the 1920s. His book *Letters on Russia* (1931) gives his generally favorable impressions of the progress made in the USSR.

5. In large Soviet apartment houses, there is a woman who sits by the elevator—not to run it, but to check who enters and leaves.

6. A northern district of Moscow, once a birch wood, where modern apartment buildings alternate with country *dachas*. It is not considered safe to walk there alone at night.

XXV

1. Alexander II's reign (1855-81) was a period of major reform in Russia, including the long-awaited emancipation of the serfs (1861), establishment of elective assemblies for local self-government and institution of public trial by jury. Reform and revolutionary movements are studied in elaborate detail in Soviet schools.

2. Felix Dzherzhinsky (1877-1926), revolutionary, Bolshevik, first director of the Cheka.

3. Joint productions with Eastern European film studios generally enjoy larger budgets and less official interference than normal. Business trips allow the traveler greater freedom than the carefully marshalled tours available, and travel abroad, even to Eastern Europe, is a privilege. Polish shoppers have a much greater selection of consumer goods at their disposal than their Russian counterparts, both in the stores and on the black market.

4. Mikhail Andreevich Suslov (b. 1902), Party and government functionary whose specialty is the continuing struggle against reactionary ideology and right- and left-deviationism.

5. Koktebel, Crimean resort. Vorkuta, coal-mining center established 1931 in the northeasternmost part of the Komi ASSR, 160 kilometers north of the Arctic Circle.

POSTSCRIPT

1. From Bella Akhmadulina's poem "The Duel" (1962), a consideration of Pushkin and Lermontov, poets "overcome by evil's paltry triumph." On the physical level, of course, Martynov killed Lermontov (1841).

2. Alexander Herzen (1812-70), journalist and political thinker, emigrated from Russia in 1847 and settled in London. In 1857, Herzen began to publish his revolutionary periodical *Kolokol (The Bell)*, which was widely read in Russia even though it had to be smuggled into the country.